Let's TALK ABOUT TRAUMA

TRAUMA

Jo Naughton

Grosvenor House
Publishing Limited

The right of Jo Naughton to be identified as the author of this
work has been asserted in accordance with Section 78
of the Copyright, Designs and Patents Act 1988

The book cover is copyright to Healed for Life

This book is published by
Grosvenor House Publishing Ltd
Link House
140 The Broadway, Tolworth, Surrey, KT6 7HT.
www.grosvenorhousepublishing.co.uk

A CIP record for this book
is available from the British Library

ISBN 978-1-83975-662-7

Some names and details have been changed to protect the
identity of the people whose stories are included in this book.
Bible references are from the New King James Version unless
otherwise stated. The Message and TPT are also used to help
reveal the heart of certain passages.

First Reviews

Terri Savelle Foy, World Renowned Speaker

Having experienced trauma first hand, Jo knows what it takes to not just to get through it, but how to experience lasting freedom and healing. In Let's Talk About Trauma, Jo will help you face the source of your pain in a gentle but powerful, Bible-based way so that you can live a restored, fear-free, and abundant life.

Prophet Tomi Arayomi, Rig Nation

Let's Talk About Trauma is a hard book to pick up, but an even harder one to put down. It is also a mirror, unlike any other, which enables the reader to identify wounds from years of emotional wear and tear, and overcome them. As an author who has navigated this terrain herself and as a gifted communicator, Jo Naughton gives us a roadmap to breakthrough. She writes as a mum, a wife, a pastor, a leader and a friend like no other. I am so grateful she has written this, it is a book that any reader will want to return to again and again.

Pastor Sola Irukwu, Jesus House

Jo Naughton is a gifted author who has written a book that speaks to the hearts of so many of us who have learned to live with traumatic experiences. Once you begin, you are immersed in each story. You consume chapter after chapter. I had my own personal encounter with the Lord and I know you will too. I felt as though I was the subject of a divinely orchestrated set-up! As I read it, the Holy Spirit shone a light on pain and turmoil.

This is a superb book which offers an invitation to the reader to embrace God's restorative power. I recommend it to anyone who desires a life of freedom and wholeness, shaped by the love of God, rather than one moulded by tragedy. Let's Talk About Trauma will change your life. It did mine!

This book is dedicated to the memory of my spiritual mother and mentor Prophet Cathy Lechner who was an unmatched example of love, humility and dignity in ministry.

Acknowledgements

Paul Naughton, thank you for being the best husband, mentor, leader and encourager I could ever have asked for.

Rita Field, thank you for your unswerving support in life and ministry and for your precious friendship, I am forever grateful to God for placing you beside me.

Terry Jackson, thank you for undergirding this much needed ministry with your love and prayers, I greatly appreciate your perseverance and commitment.

Robert & Joicie Rivera, thank you for being my second home on the other side of the pond, and for your unceasing labor of love in ministry.

Tim Collins, thank you for investing your time and talents into this ministry. Both your wisdom and your way with words are a tremendous blessing.

Freisa Dávila, your creativity is phenomenal! Thank you for helping me every step of the way to communicate powerfully with pictures.

Contents

Chapter 1

THE TRUTH ABOUT TRAUMA

Veronica was working in a central London hospital when the lethal COVID 19 pandemic spread like wildfire across the British capital. Seriously ill men and women filled every available hospital bed and wards nearly split at the seams. Staff were covered from head to toe in highly protective clothing in an attempt to keep the deadly virus away. Although the gloves, visors and overalls were vital for staff safety, the sight was almost apocalyptic and very disturbing. Veronica was looking after patients who were fighting for every breath. Ventilators whirred, alarms sounded, and thudding footsteps hurried towards critically sick people. What made things even worse was watching patients arrive sick, then stabilizing, before suddenly getting much worse. Death was a daily event. This normally calm London hospital looked like something out of a horror movie.

Working double shifts, often without breaks, Veronica would come home only to shower, snatch a couple of hours of sleep, and then return to the frontline. Soon the trauma of this war against death took its toll. Veronica was suffering under the intense pressure. She explained, "I was living on a knife edge. Stressed, stretched and terrified of making even the tiniest mistake, I became completely overwhelmed. I was tense during the little time that I had at home, which affected my family too. I struggled to sleep."

Trauma cripples. Even seemingly insignificant events can leave us shaken. More often than not, we don't understand the damage done

1

and try to put it all behind us. Sometimes we end up with irrational fears. Violence that we experience whilst growing up can produce anger or constant nervousness. A distressing trip to the dentist can make you anxious in other medical settings. A car crash might leave you scared of driving. On other occasions, we adapt our routines so that we don't have to look back at unpleasant memories. Maybe you avoid a particular town or talking to new people. Perhaps you change the subject if someone mentions a certain season or you look away when you pass a hospital. It is staggering how many of us have phobias or fears that control our lives.

Trauma can even shape personalities. Babies are not born shy. Distressing experiences open the door to intimidation. A short fuse, oversensitivity, passive-aggressive tendencies, emotional detachment or harshness are examples of traits that are often borne out of distress. Even our preferences can be influenced by unpleasant events. You might not like hugs, going on holiday, being photographed or making telephone calls. Perhaps you think it's just the way you are, but aversions like these are often forged by pain. Romans 8:14 tells us that God's children should be led by His Spirit, not shaped by trauma.

IT HAPPENS TO US ALL

There are many causes of trauma; from accidents, medical procedures and illnesses, to abuse, violence and unexpected loss. It is not always what you go through yourself. Sometimes it is what you witness that marks your life. It might be a child at the top of the stairs watching their parents fight or a soldier seeing atrocities. Irrespective of what caused the distress, what all these experiences have in common is their ability to cause lasting damage. It is only when our hearts are healed that we can completely defuse trauma's impact on our lives.

Sometimes seemingly insignificant events shape the way we live. Towards the end of 2019, I came across an online course that could help us raise awareness of our ministry Healed for Life.

It was a simple formula for gaining media coverage, so I enrolled. As I worked my way through the program, I realized that I would need to pitch ideas for articles to journalists. Although I knew this was an excellent idea, even the thought of talking to the media made me intensely uncomfortable.

I know enough about the human heart to understand the importance of questioning illogical negative emotion, so I enquired of the Lord. I used a prayer which I call 'Rebekah's Request' and is recorded in the book of Genesis. Isaac's wife Rebekah was pregnant, but something didn't feel right. We don't know if she was in pain or just churning inside. She went to the Lord and prayed a powerful prayer: "If all is well then why am I like this?" (Genesis 25:22). The Lord revealed the reason for Rebekah's inner struggle: she was carrying twins. As I have done many times before when my emotions have made no sense, I asked the Lord, "If all is well, then why am I like this? Why am I uncomfortable contacting journalists?"

The Holy Spirit took me back to my first job after graduating. Three memories came to mind, in quick succession. In truth, they are trivial, but they powerfully demonstrate the impact of seemingly insignificant experiences... My first assignment as a junior PR executive was to make a series of phone calls to fire departments. "Say you are a student conducting academic research," my boss instructed me. I had to make twenty phone calls and lie twenty times. I was distressed by this assignment but said nothing to anyone. That is, until God took me back to the memory thirty years later. I realized how fraudulent I felt telling lie after lie to complete strangers. I was afraid of being found out, and a dislike of making telephone calls settled in my heart.

FEELING LIKE A FOOL

The second memory was from about a year later while I was working for the same company. One of our clients was a dog food manufacturer that had a major presence at a big British dog show.

Our company was charged with generating media coverage for them at the event. This was always a challenge because all the brands at the show wanted a piece of the PR action. Our agency came up with a series of creative ideas to attract the attention of journalists and photographers. One involved me...

My boss told me that I looked like a yellow Labrador dog. Aware that the media look for quirky pictures, she asked me to attend the dog show wearing a branded tee shirt and a short skirt. When I arrived, I was instructed to hunt for a yellow Labrador sleeping in a kennel. "Ask the permission of the owner," I was told. "Then climb in beside the dog and pretend to sleep." They were hoping that a photographer would spot me sleeping beside the lookalike dog and that branded pictures would appear in the press. I was mortified but obeyed my boss's instructions. I can still remember walking around the kennels with a knot in my stomach seeking the right breed and then lying down. Time passed very slowly but thankfully no photographers passed by. Afterwards, I laughed it off, but a fear of the media got buried in my heart.

FORGOTTEN MEMORIES

The third memory was a few months after the experience at the dog show. I was asked to give a presentation to a group of managers and journalists at an event in a hotel. At the end of a successful evening, I headed to my room. I stepped into the elevator with a group of colleagues and clients. A senior client (who was old enough to be my father) got off at my floor and followed me. I assumed his room was near mine. When I reached my door, he asked if he could come in for a coffee.

Unfortunately, I was both naive and accommodating. Although I was anxious, I agreed. I walked through the door, showed him the sofa and went to make him a hot drink. As I walked over, he grabbed the cup from my hand, shelved it, then pushed me backwards onto the bed. He threw himself on top of me, trying to kiss and touch me. He pinned me down. I swung my head from side to side, desperate to avoid his face. I kicked and shouted until he eventually relented. My client thrust me off and left the room accusing me of being a slut. I dusted myself off and put it behind me, but a dislike for media relations grew in my heart.

As God brought me back to the pain and the shame, I wept for a few minutes over each memory. I told the Lord how each event made me feel and He healed my heart. I realized that my real fear was not about talking to journalists. I was afraid of being made to feel like a fraud. I was scared of being humiliated for the sake of media coverage, and I was fearful of being stripped of my dignity in the presence of the press. Somehow my heart had associated these three unhealed memories with pitching to journalists. Jeremiah 17:9-10 (AMPC) explains: "The heart is deceitful above all things... Who can know it [perceive, understand, be acquainted with his own heart and mind]? I the Lord search..." I had no idea that these unresolved issues were hiding in my heart. When I asked the Lord to explain my aversions, He revealed the contents of my soul.

My twenty something year old heart had buried these memories and the fears they generated. These were minor traumas, but each experience shook me enough to shape my behavior. Firstly, I developed a dislike of making telephone calls. Any time I needed to contact folk, I would email or text. I wonder how many needy people I neglected to call because of my unresolved issues. Perhaps there were times when I needed help, but I did not pick up the telephone because I was uncomfortable. A seemingly insignificant experience influenced my behavior for three decades.

Secondly, I disliked approaching the media. The thought of contacting a journalist made me extremely uneasy. I avoided anything that reminded me of public relations and even moved out of that specialism and into marketing. For years, I was hardly even aware of this and put it down to personal preferences. Distressing experiences had dictated my decisions when I should have been following the leading of the Holy Spirit. Trauma changes us, yet when we are healed, any associated phobias dissolve.

WHAT IS TRAUMA?

A bodily trauma is a wound or shock produced by sudden physical injury. An emotional trauma is our response to a distressing experience such as an accident, attack or even a natural disaster. Trauma is different to other types of pain. It is usually shocking and disturbing. Immediately afterwards, we are often in disbelief or denial. Sometimes we bury the pain because it is too hard to handle. We work overtime to forget what we went through and try to get on with our lives. That might sound sensible, but buried wounds don't vanish. Time does not heal. Jesus does.

How do we know if we have buried trauma? In short, we often don't know until the Holy Spirit reveals it. I had no idea that pockets of pain were trapped in my soul until I asked God why I was wary of journalists. I did not know that my dislike of making telephone calls was the result of an uncomfortable experience. We need the Holy Spirit to reveal what's hiding deep inside. However, there are also telltale signs. Just as a cough and a fever are symptoms of a virus, so there are some clear indicators of unresolved trauma.

SYMPTOMS

Some signs of trauma are more obvious than others. You may think you are relatively unaffected by the events of your life, but perhaps you recognize some of these symptoms... Do you get anxious in certain settings? Can particular sights or smells make you feel uncomfortable? Does the mention of a specific name or town make you churn inside? Maybe you grab the seat in fright when you are being driven or perhaps you grip the steering wheel yourself in certain situations. You may have flashbacks that can send you into a spin.

Do people tell you that you have a short fuse? Maybe you realize that you easily get angry. All may be well, and everything could be calm, but then suddenly you snap. It might be a broken plate or a loud noise that causes you to lash out. If someone you love is late home, does your heart race until they return? If that's you, I encourage you to get my book Lifting the Mask where I deal with this issue. You could get easily irritated by inconsequential events. You might think that's just your personality, but these are typical traits of a person who has been affected by trauma.

The list of symptoms continues. Maybe you withdraw from other people? You need to be alone, but then often end up feeling isolated. Perhaps you feel disconnected from your own emotions, as though everything happened to someone else. Maybe you are just numb. Alternatively, you could have inexplicable mood swings. You're up one minute, then you sink into sadness. You could have difficulty concentrating or you could easily get confused. You may find that mental functions are taxing. Finally, you could have a sense of hopelessness. You just don't know how to get the change that you so desperately need. As a result, despondency sets in.

THE ENEMY'S PURPOSE FOR YOUR PAIN

The symptoms are varied and unpleasant, yet it is the ultimate impact of trauma that is most concerning. Left unchecked, trauma can derail your destiny. A few years ago, my daughter had an accident. At the time, I was in America ministering. My husband Paul called me to let me know that Abby had fallen off her bike and hurt her wrist. I was due to fly home the following evening so although I was upset to be so far away, I reassured myself that I would be home soon. I arrived back two days later. Once safely home, my husband called me and asked if I was sitting down. Paul had very thoughtfully withheld the full facts to protect me. Now that I was back home, he told me exactly what had happened...

Abby had been cycling downhill in the woods at about 25 miles an hour when she must have hit a rock. She was thrown off her bicycle. An ambulance reached the scene at about the same time my husband arrived. Covered in blood, Abby was rushed to the emergency room. She had broken her jaw in two places and needed multiple stitches all over her face. And yes, she also fractured her wrist. I will never forget the moment that my husband brought my daughter home from the hospital. Paul brought Abby into our living room where I was sitting. However hard I searched; I could not see my little girl. Abby's face was so swollen and disfigured that she was unrecognizable. She could only see out of a tiny slit in one eye. I sat with her on the sofa for hours.

Apart from the agony of seeing my daughter disfigured and in so much pain, one other thing was eating away at me. I was not there when Abby needed me the most. I could not imagine how frightened she must have felt. Girls need their mothers, especially when things go wrong. However, I was thousands of miles away. My husband had to handle the whole trauma alone. I felt terrible, but because I was not the one who was hurt, I belittled my distress. Maybe that's your story: someone else's agony has traumatized you. Please don't dismiss your need to be healed. Watching someone you love suffer is sometimes more difficult than handling your own pain. I got into God's presence and told the Lord how much it had hurt to see my daughter in such distress. Yet that wasn't the issue that was eating me away on the inside. Eventually, I told the Lord the painful truth: "I wasn't there when my daughter needed me!" I cried while God healed my heart.

We are better equipped to help others when we have dealt with our own pain. As they say on airplane safety videos, "Fix your own mask before helping anyone else with theirs." As I left the presence of the Lord, my heart was at peace and I could support my daughter's recovery. However, that wasn't the reason for me sharing this story.

THE PROBLEM WITH PAIN

God has called me to establish our ministry in the United States. I said at the start that I was not there when Abby had the accident because I was in America. I have no doubt that if I had not dealt with my sense of guilt, I would have become anxious about traveling and particularly concerned about going to the USA. I can imagine that I would have worried about my family's wellbeing. Because I was healed, fear lost its grip, and I was free to follow the leading of the Holy Spirit. I returned to America within a couple of weeks with no worry.

The devil has a purpose for your pain. He wants to use it to keep you from the people who God has called you to help. Maybe you were attacked in a certain city where the Lord has called you to work. Perhaps you were ridiculed over your passions and so you changed the direction of your life. You could have been humiliated by people from a certain nation, so you now avoid those who you are gifted to help. The enemy wants you to bunker down and become wary. He wants you to put up walls and harden your heart. Unhealed trauma is a powerful destiny-wrecker.

Psalms 84:5-7: "Blessed is the man whose strength is in You, whose heart is set on pilgrimage. As they pass through the Valley of Baca, they make it a spring; the rain also covers it with pools. They go from strength to strength; each one appears before God in Zion." When you are on a pilgrimage, you are on a journey. Baca is the Hebrew for weeping. I encourage you to commit to your healing journey. It will probably take you through places of pain, but it will lead you out the other side in strength. As you allow the Lord to highlight any hidden hurts, He will bring healing and freedom. You will then be ready to arise and fulfill every ounce of your God-given purpose. Let's pray.

Heavenly Father,

I ask You to take me on a life-changing journey as I read. Holy Spirit, please shine Your light into the depths of my heart and reveal any trauma hidden inside. Expose trapped pain that is holding me back. I open up my soul to You and I ask You to have Your way in me.

If the Lord has already started to expose sadness within, please pray: Lord, thank You for helping me to see how I have been hurt. I don't want that pain buried any longer. I ask You to help me to bring it to You. (*Now tell the Lord about the memory or memories that have surfaced. Tell Him what happened and how it made you feel. Be as specific as possible.*) Heal my heart, I pray, Oh Lord. Take my pain away. Lord, I ask You to pour Your wonderful love into the place where I was once wounded. I receive Your perfect peace.

In Jesus' name, I pray,

Amen.

CAUSES

Trauma comes in all shapes and sizes. Sometimes it is blindingly obvious, but on other occasions it goes unnoticed. However it happens, trauma harms us so we need to be healed. In the next few chapters, the Lord will reveal pain hidden in your heart and He will expose fear that has kept you bound. As you read, allow the Holy Spirit to shine His light deep within your soul. What He brings back to your memory, He will heal.

Chapter 2

INJURY

After an intense night of labor, the baby's crown began to show. This is the time that every mother has to push with all of her might! As the head eventually emerged, the midwife shouted abruptly, "Stop pushing!" The atmosphere instantly changed in the hospital room. The emergency team crashed through the doors as my midwife quickly cut the cord which was wrapped twice around our child's neck. The little one was born grey and lifeless. "Go with the baby!" I cried to my husband as he ran out with the medical team.

I was left alone with a nurse. "Did I have a boy or a girl?" I asked. "I'm sorry," she responded. "I didn't check." I lay motionless on a bed in the birthing room while she went to get news. About twenty minutes later, the midwife returned and explained, "You had a little girl, but we really don't know if she will make it." Our daughter had been starved of oxygen for ten long minutes. Each time I pushed; the cord had tightened around her neck. She was being suffocated with every contraction. The medics were now working tirelessly to resuscitate our little one. I was soon wheeled into a side room for post birth treatment. As a doctor worked on me, I cried out in my heart, "What is it about me and girls?" It was just two years earlier that my husband and I had lost our first child Naomi to meningitis.

Eventually, I was taken to a private bedroom to recover and wait for news. When medics suspect that a baby will die, they take photographs while the child is alive so that the parents have a memento. A couple of pictures were brought to my bedside which I pored over and treasured. Two hours after our baby was born, I was told that she was alive. However, I was also informed that the first 24 hours would be touch and go, and that if she did make it, they would not be able to detect the level of brain damage for at least a day after that.

FIRST IMPRESSIONS

I hadn't yet seen my little girl so the nurses helped me into a wheelchair so that I could visit her in neonatal intensive care. They brought me to an incubator where I saw a tiny baby fighting for her life. She was wired up to breathing apparatus and monitors, surrounded by flashing lights and strange whirring noises. After a sleepless night and the exhaustion of labor, it was too much for me. Overwhelmed, I asked the kind nurse to wheel me back to my room.

Abby was born on a Sunday morning, so my husband messaged every church leader he knew asking for prayer. Thousands of Christians across London lifted up our little girl and our faithful God answered! Contrary to doctors' expectations, Abby made a full recovery, and we brought our little princess home from hospital ten days after she was born. Tests even showed that her brain was functioning normally! Abby was well, but I had been traumatized.

When a storm is over, there is often a temptation to bury the pain. We want to turn away from any memory that may take us back to the trauma. Somehow, even as intelligent adults, we convince ourselves that ignoring an issue will make it go away. It is illogical to think that a squatter will leave your house if you ignore him. Pain is real. Just as physical wounds need to be treated to reduce the risk of lasting damage, so emotional pain must be healed to ensure our future well-being.

GETTING AWAY FROM IT ALL

There are some experiences we think we can ignore. However, a return to places or people who remind us of the past can result in emotional reactions. Until I was healed of the trauma of my daughter's birth, hospitals seemed like unpleasant places, midwives appeared formidable, and certain smells and sounds triggered anxiety. After my heart was healed, I could return to hospitals - even in emergencies - without anxiety. I could hear the sounds that once made me recoil and be completely unmoved. We know that we have been healed of trauma because telltale sights, sounds or smells are no longer emotional triggers. We can be at peace in the midst of circumstances that would once have caused turmoil.

The Bible is powerful, yet we must believe what it says if we want to experience its promises. For years, I tried to convince myself that I believed Psalms 139:14, which says: "I will praise You, for I am fearfully and wonderfully made; marvelous are Your works, and that my soul knows very well." Experiences that I had whilst growing up made me believe that I was worthless, so it was hard for me to accept that I was fearfully and wonderfully made. However, when the Lord started to heal me of buried pain, it became easy to believe that I was God's precious handiwork.

In the same way, after you have had the wounds of trauma dealt with, you will have a different outlook on life. It will be easier to enjoy His peace and drive out all fear. The verses that follow reveal the way it feels after you have been healed: "He will cover you with His pinions, and under His wings shall you trust and find refuge; His truth and His faithfulness are a shield and a buckler. You shall not be afraid of the terror of the night, nor of the arrow (the evil plots and slanders of the wicked) that flies by day, nor of the pestilence that stalks in darkness, nor of the destruction and sudden death that surprise and lay waste at noonday." (Psalms 91:4-6 AMPC). In short, healing brings a calm to your heart.

DROPPED

A little boy who suffered terribly is introduced to us in 2 Samuel 4:4 (NLT): "Saul's son Jonathan had a son named Mephibosheth, who was crippled as a child. He was five years old when the report came from Jezreel that Saul and Jonathan had been killed in battle. When the child's nurse heard the news, she picked him up and fled. But as she hurried away, she dropped him, and he became crippled."

This five-year-old child was raised during a brutal civil war. One day, there was a sudden frenzy; everyone was running for their life. Mephibosheth had a nurse who was supposed to protect and care for him. I imagine that he loved and trusted this lady. However, in the chaos and confusion, the nurse dropped the little boy as she ran. It must have been a nasty fall because he broke both his feet. We don't know how many bones were fractured or if there was much blood. I'm sure that the little lad screamed in agony, but his cries were probably drowned out by the shouts all around. Unable to get help, his nurse must have picked him back up and carried on running. Mephibosheth received no medication or professional help. He was crippled by the accident at a time when disability was seen as a scourge.

That fall completely changed Mephibosheth's life. He no longer saw himself as a member of the royal family (remember, his grandfather was King Saul). He now saw himself as a worthless animal. He was marked by this childhood trauma. Many years later, King David asked to see Mephibosheth, so the young man was brought before the king. We will pick up the story in 2 Samuel 9:7-8 (NLT): "'Don't be afraid!' David said. "I intend to show kindness to you because of my promise to your father, Jonathan. I will give you all the property that once belonged to your grandfather Saul, and you will eat here with me at the king's table!' Mephibosheth bowed... and exclaimed, "Who is your servant, that you should show such kindness to a dead dog like me?"'

DEAD DOG

Mephibosheth's body was not working properly, but that was not his biggest problem. He felt worthless. Proverbs 23:7 says, "As a man thinks in his heart, so is he..." Our deep-seated beliefs influence our decisions and actions. Mephibosheth believed that his physical limitations diminished his value. It would have been bad enough if he had seen himself as an animal, but it was worse than that. He saw himself as a *dead* dog. I don't know what you have been through that has squashed your view of your value. Maybe you were scarred in an accident, or perhaps you have a life-limiting medical condition. It could be that your issues aren't physical. Maybe your memory or thinking skills have been damaged. Perhaps a disease has left you with embarrassing or painful problems. It's easy to focus so much on physical ailments that we forget to take care of the damage to our hearts.

Proverbs 4:23 (NLT) says, "Guard your heart above all else, for it determines the course of your life." Your inner image shapes your expectations. If Mephibosheth had understood his value, he would have been ready to receive the blessings that David wanted to pour into his life. However, his wounded soul caused him to resist the kindness of the king. He did not believe that he deserved to be treated like royalty. He thought that his issues belittled his worth. Mephibosheth obviously hated himself. He thought that he was disgusting. This prince was God's precious creation, but Mephibosheth rejected himself.

WHAT ABOUT YOU?

If you look down on yourself as a result of any limitation, the Lord wants to heal your heart. Jeremiah 30:17 reveals the compassion of God for people who have been made to feel worthless: "'I will restore health to you and heal you of your wounds,' says the LORD, "Because they called you an outcast, saying: "This is Zion; no one seeks her."'" When we are made to feel like an outcast, it hurts. Perhaps you were ridiculed for your appearance or made to feel ashamed of your body. Maybe the actions of others led you to see yourself as damaged goods. You may feel unwanted. God saw Israel's pain and He sees how you have been hurt. The Lord promised to heal their hearts and His desire is to restore you too, from the inside out.

Unfortunately, a sense of shame can cause us to hide from these sorts of hurts. We don't want to admit that we see ourselves as inadequate because the truth is too painful. However, it is important that you go to the Lord and share the deep issues of your heart with Him. In Lamentations 1:20, Jeremiah poured out his pain in prayer: "See, O Lord, that I am in distress; My soul is troubled; My heart is overturned within me..." The temptation to bury pain can be overwhelming. Please resist for the sake of your future. As God heals your heart, your life will become so much more enjoyable.

WREAKING HAVOC

With her eight-month-old baby in her arms and her feet pressed firmly against the bathroom door, Jane did what she could to protect herself and her child as the storm raged overhead. After everything died down, Jane cautiously opened the bathroom door that had kept them safe. Nothing could have prepared her for what she saw: the wind had ripped the roof off their home. There was shattered glass everywhere. In a daze, Jane picked up her baby and walked down her street to see devastation in every direction. Trees had collapsed on houses; cars were overturned and all forms of power were down. Hurricane Andrew had destroyed Jane's home, her neighborhood and much of her state.

When entire communities suffer together, individuals may feel unable to deal with their pain. "I made it out alive, so who am I to complain? My neighbor was hit harder, so I should be grateful," we say to ourselves. Let me explain something. Getting out alive does not stop calamity from being traumatic.

Someone else suffering more severe injuries does not stop the experience from hurting you. Imagine if a person with a broken arm refused to go to the emergency room at the scene of an accident because one man had been killed and another was in a critical condition. We need to treat physical wounds irrespective of their severity. In the same way, we need to be healed of *all* emotional pain. Please don't allow guilt of any sort to keep you from your own recovery.

WHEN EVERYTHING FALLS APART

When everything around you seems to be falling apart, it can create a deep sense of insecurity. It can also make you feel alone. Maybe you have seen terrible atrocities in war, or perhaps you lived through riots or street violence. When life itself feels unsafe, it is important that we remind ourselves about the strength of the God that we serve. Deuteronomy 33:27 (NLT) says, "The eternal God is your refuge, and His everlasting arms are under you." If you have been shaken by one of life's storms, I encourage you to shut your eyes right now and picture His strong arms around you upholding you. Your Heavenly Father has your back, as Isaiah 52:12b says, "...the God of Israel will be your rear guard."

In the months after the hurricane, the Lord restored Jane's heart so that future storms did not create undue anxiety. One way we know that we have been healed is by our ability to calmly face sights, sounds and smells that once triggered adverse reactions. Healing takes the sting out of unpleasant memories. If you realize that some of your reactions to life's knocks are disproportionate, you probably need to be healed. For example, if you jump when a balloon bursts or if you miss a heartbeat when an ambulance passes, ask the Lord to restore your soul. When you can look back on events that used to cause you to cower and now view them without any negative emotion, you are well on your way to wholeness.

A VIOLENT SHAKING

Trapped in her Los Angeles hotel room on the twenty-fourth floor, an eerie growling coupled with a violent shaking woke Maria in the early hours of the morning. Disorientated, she jumped out of bed just as the rocking started. Maria grabbed her mattress to keep herself from falling as the entire building swayed. Water in the swimming pool sloshed from side to side like liquid in a washing up bowl. Maria realized it was an earthquake. Not knowing what might happen next, Maria made it to the bathroom where she lay in the tub for protection in case the building collapsed. As soon as it became clear that the worst was over, she packed her things, cut short her trip and headed home.

The tremors and rocking that night only lasted for minutes, but the trauma gripped Maria for months. Even the slightest turbulence on a flight caused Maria to jump in fright. When she lay down beside her children at night, even a slight movement would cause her to cry out in terror. It was not just LA that was shook up that day. Maria was also shaken to the core.

One of trauma's cruel hallmarks is its capacity to make its victims feel unsafe. The shock of the calamity can leave us reeling for months and even years. If you have been through a frightening experience, please don't belittle the negative impact it may have had. The fact that you are okay now is wonderful, but you may still need to recover from emotional trauma. Either way, I encourage you to ask the Holy Spirit to give you a fresh revelation of the Lord as your *safe place*. No matter what is happening, remember what Jesus promised in Hebrews 13:5a-6: "I will never leave you nor forsake you." He will never let you down. He is your refuge.

Jesus told us to become like a child (see Matthew 18:3). Even as adults, we will always be children in the sight of God. Just as a child would rush to their parents in the face of danger, we need to run to our Heavenly Father. Psalms 61:2-4 (NLT) says, "From the ends of the earth, I cry to You for help when my heart is overwhelmed. Lead me to the towering rock of safety, for You are my safe refuge, a fortress where my enemies cannot reach me. Let me live forever in Your sanctuary, safe beneath the shelter of your wings!" He has your life in His hands. He is your safe place.

DAZED BY THE SMASH

Motoring back from a mall on the outskirts of Atlanta, my friends and I laughed as we chatted. We were traveling at about fifty miles an hour along a state route when a big car suddenly smashed into the side of our cab. Time froze as we ground to a halt. We were silenced by shock as smoke filled the car. Aware even in that moment that I was in the company of esteemed ministers, I politely enquired, "Do you think we should probably get out of this vehicle before it, er... explodes?" Brought back into the moment, we all clambered out of the car in a daze.

Disoriented but with no major injuries, we viewed the extent of the damage. One of the pastors observed: "One inch to the left and this vehicle would have jack-knifed." I didn't appreciate the significance of this statement at the time but gathered from his tone that we had narrowly escaped disaster. Due at the Christian TV network TBN's studios a couple of hours later, we hurried to arrange alternative transport back to our hotel. We had fifteen minutes to shower, change and then jump back into a car. I put on some jewelry and applied my make-up on the way to the studios.

Arriving at TBN, we kept our misadventure to ourselves. We taped the show in front of a live studio audience and then headed back to the hotel, still shaken. I went to bed that night exhausted. When I woke up, the trauma caught up with me. I closed my eyes and talked with our Wonderful Counsellor (see Isaiah 9:6) about my ordeal. "Last night was terrible, Lord. The sudden smash, the smell of smoke. It was horrendous..." I burst into tears as I told my Heavenly Father that I was afraid and shaken. After a few minutes of pouring out my pain, I felt the peace of God fill my heart.

FACING IT HEAD-ON

Mine was a minor accident. Maybe you have been in a horrific crash. Perhaps you witnessed fatalities. You could have seen a horrible incident at work or at home. If we don't deal with the shock, it will probably have repercussions. Maybe your heart races whenever you see a car's headlights shining in your rear-view mirror. Perhaps you start to sweat when you overtake. Maybe the sight of stairways, hospitals or racing ambulances leaves you shaken. When trauma remains unhealed, it has a habit of hampering our lives. Whatever the experience, we need to have zero tolerance of trauma in our hearts.

Shock can be overwhelming. Although we might not see the full impact immediately, it often catches up with us, leaving us winded. We need to bring every trauma, however insignificant, to the Lord in prayer. When we talk to our loving Lord about our experiences, the trauma breaks. Listen to the way David shared his heart with the Lord in Psalms 124:4-7 (NLT): "The waters would have engulfed us; a torrent would have overwhelmed us. Yes, the raging waters of their fury would have overwhelmed our very lives. Praise the Lord, who did not let their teeth tear us apart! We escaped like a bird from a hunter's trap. The trap is broken, and we are free!" As the king opened up in the presence of God, the intimidation disappeared, and he found freedom.

WITNESSING DEVASTATION

It took Noah about seventy-five years to build the Ark, but I don't think anything could have prepared him for the flood that destroyed the earth. I know that he and his family were tightly shut inside, but nature's ferocity as well as the knowledge of so much human suffering must have been terrible. Genesis 7:11b

LET'S TALK ABOUT TRAUMA

describes the moment disaster struck: "...On that day all the fountains of the great deep were broken up, and the windows of heaven were opened."

Noah had preached - probably for years - about this, but no one listened. I wonder if the faces of old friends or neighbors flashed through his mind. As well as handling the catastrophe at a personal level, he must have felt a weight of responsibility for his wife, sons and daughters-in-law. Of course, they will have been forever grateful for being saved, but I can't imagine that they were untouched by the human tragedy.

WHAT HAVE YOU SEEN?

Seeing others suffer can be even harder than enduring pain yourself. You may have seen your brothers in arms suffer terribly, or you could have watched while your community was devastated by violence or sickness. As a parent, perhaps you have watched your child face agonizing medical procedures. As a husband or wife, you might have seen your spouse broken by trauma. It could be that you witnessed family or friends endure terrible pain. You may have been the first at the scene of a terrible accident and the images still haunt you.

It can be dreadful to feel helpless when witnessing the pain of others. Please don't dismiss the importance of being restored after 'second-hand' trauma. Although you were not the one who went through the agony, if you want to help others, you need to be at peace yourself. Jesus put it this way: "Can the blind lead the blind? Will they not both fall into the ditch?" (Luke 6:39). When your heart is free of pain, you can be full of faith for the restoration of others.

Have you ever considered that your Heavenly Father understands? The Bible tells us how God feels when we are heartbroken. Jeremiah 8:21 says, "For the hurt of the daughter of my people I am hurt. I am mourning..." The Lord is hurt when we are hurt, just as you are pained when you see someone you care about suffer. What is the buried sadness of your soul? What are the regrets hiding in your heart? You can say it all in God's presence. You can tell Him what you couldn't tell anyone else. God feels your pain and wants to heal your heart.

THE UNCOMFORTABLE TRUTH

Very often, the reason we get weighed down is that we can't bring ourselves to say the one thing that is heaviest on our hearts. The truth can be painful. However, it is always the way to freedom. When Abby suffered that horrible cycling accident I described in chapter one, I felt a terrible guilt. After all, I was not there when my family needed me the most. I was sure that my little girl needed her mother and that my husband needed his wife by his side. I felt like I had failed. For hours, I had a knot in my stomach, unable to admit (even to myself) my guilt. I looked at my daughter's terrible injuries and sat with her in silence.

Eventually, I took myself to my room and fell on my knees in God's presence. I pushed the painful truth out of my mouth. "Lord, I was not there when my precious little girl needed me. I left my husband to handle the crisis alone." I cried in prayer, then left His presence in peace. I was now able to join my faith with my husband's for her complete healing. Do you have any guilt or regret hiding in your heart? Do you feel like you let down someone you love? Are you embarrassed about what happened or do you feel shame for some sort of failure? The only way that you and I can be our best when it matters most is if we deal with hidden heart issues. Ephesians 5:13 says that anything that is exposed to the light becomes light. When any type of discomfort is hidden in our hearts, it has the power to pull us down. Once we bring it into the light, it loses its grip.

When I came out of my prayer closet, I sat again with my daughter. Although it was difficult, I now had the courage to say what I couldn't admit before. It is always better to be real with God before we open our hearts with people. With a new calm in my heart, I spoke to my daughter: "Abby, I am so sorry that I was not there when you needed me." My big deal might sound like nothing to you but it was a mountain to me. I was peering through a tiny crack in my daughter's eye. Although she couldn't speak or eat, she somehow managed to reply, "I didn't need you, Mummy. Daddy was amazing." My husband also told me that they managed fine without me. I was blown away. To be honest, I was ready for anything because of God's healing balm, but her response and his reassurance refreshed my soul.

HEAVENLY CLOSURE

We don't often get that kind of human closure. However, we can always get a heavenly perspective. It demands the kind of honesty which is referenced in Psalm 51:6: "Behold, You desire truth in the inner being..." (Amplified). If you feel guilty that someone else was hurt in your place, it's time to tell the Lord. If you feel at fault for their pain, or even for your pain, you need to open your mouth and confide in your Wonderful Counselor. When we pour out our pain or guilt, when we share the truth about how we really feel, He lifts our burdens and heals our hearts.

Whatever ways trauma has affected your life, the Lord wants you to be free. In truth, we have all been winded and shocked at different points in our lives. It is vital that you ask the Lord to deal with the damage so that you can rise up strong. I don't know what you have been through, but the Lord knows. If there is any pain buried in you from accidents, disasters, appointments, crashes, procedures or any other type of injury, the Lord wants to do a work in your life. As I said earlier, I will share the steps to healing in section three. For now, I encourage you to ask the Lord to uncover what's hidden so that you are ready to heal. Before we pray, use the Trauma Tracker on the next page to help identify any hidden trauma.

INJURY TRAUMA TRACKER

Use the list below to identify any traumatic events you have experienced or witnessed. Put a check mark beside each category that is relevant to you and then write one adjective beside the event that best describes how you feel when you think about that experience. Ask the Holy Spirit to help you to complete the checklist.

☐ Animal bites or stings _____

☐ Bicycle accident _____

☐ Car accident _____

☐ Dental incident _____

☐ Earthquake _____

☐ Fall _____

☐ Flood _____

☐ Hospital horror _____

☐ Hurricane _____

☐ Medical problem _____

☐ Medical procedure _____

☐ Motorcycle accident _____

☐ Storm _____

☐ Workplace accident _____

☐ Other _____

Take note of any negative emotions which are stirred up as a result of thinking about old experiences. Distress, discomfort, regret, sadness, angst, disquiet or any other negative reaction is an indication that you still need to be healed. In Chapter Eight, you will be able to come back to this list as an aid to your healing. Let's pray:

Heavenly Father,

My heart's desire is to fulfill every ounce of my God-given potential, so I don't want any trauma buried in my soul. I want to be completely healed so that I can live life to the full. Where I have dismissed the importance of being restored, I ask for Your forgiveness. (*If you know that you have glossed over emotional damage, tell the Lord that you are sorry for ignoring those wounds.*)

Where I have deliberately hardened my heart to hide pain, I ask that You would tenderize my soul instead. (*If you know that you have toughened up as a defense mechanism, tell the Lord when and why and ask Him to soften your heart.*)

If I have adapted my behavior or dodged certain people or places to avoid facing wounds, I am sorry, Lord. I ask for Your help to deal with any hidden hurt. Lord, please uncover any underlying issues so that I can be free.

If I have pushed down pain because it was too unpleasant, I ask for Your forgiveness and I ask for Your help to feel so that I can be healed. If I have been hurt as a result of seeing those I love suffer, I ask that You would uncover those wounds so that I may be healed.

My heart is open before You, Lord. Have Your way in me.

In Jesus' name, I pray,

Amen.

Chapter 3

CRUELTY

"As I greeted my father, his eyes filled with tears," Helen explained. "He hesitantly reached out and put an arm around me. He kept asking, 'Is that really you?' Trembling, he whispered, 'I never thought I'd see you again.' He thanked me over and over again. I didn't even feel as though anything had ever happened all those years ago. The memories of the past had been wiped away from the deep places of my heart. My healing journey brought remarkable restoration to my heart."

HELEN'S CHILDHOOD HELL

Helen was eight years old the first time she was raped. Her dad entered her room one night and forced himself on her. He didn't say a word, then left as abruptly as he had arrived. Curled up in a ball under her tiny desk, she cried herself to sleep. Helen's father went on to rape her continuously for the next six years. She once tried to protect herself by tying her shorts more tightly than ever, but this backfired. He ripped them off and then raped her anyway.

Helen tried to make him stop: "I would plead: 'Please don't. I will wash the dishes better. I will iron the clothes without creases. I will do anything to make you stop.' But he never answered. After he left me, I would shake - sometimes for hours. I felt disgusted and would use a floor scrubber to try to scrape the dirt and shame away. Then I would cry myself to sleep."

BATTERED

It wasn't just sexual abuse. From as early as she could remember, Helen's dad hit her. He would beat her if she didn't fold the clothes properly, if she didn't do the dishes right and if she took too long getting home from school. He would whip her with his belt, leaving her back and chest covered in bruises. He was careful to avoid her face so nobody would know.

Then there were his words. Helen's dad crushed her confidence one comment at a time: "You're too ugly to be my daughter, you will never achieve anything, you are disgusting". She believed she was worthless. Helen's father had a different woman every six months. One after another, she begged them to stay, but they all left because he abused them too. He never allowed Helen to have friends and told her that he knew where she was and what she was doing at all times. She was terrified.

THE IMPACT

Years later, Helen met a wonderful man and got married. On the surface, life looked fine, but she had deep problems. Helen didn't have any real friends. She would not allow anybody in, ever. If anything went wrong, she felt rejected. Helen was afraid of leaders and teachers, she was afraid of failing, and she was ashamed of every part of her body. She explained, "When I saw a scar, I remembered how it happened. I felt dirty. I thought I was worthless as a mother, worthless as a woman and worthless as a human being."

After about three years of marriage, Helen's husband begged her to get help. That's when she attended our two-day conference, Healed for Life. During one of the sessions, the Holy Spirit took her back to her childhood. She saw her dad standing in front of her and she broke down. She poured out her heart like water in the presence of the Lord. She went to bed after day one, but wept all night long. She could hardly see in the morning because she had cried for hours. "At the end of Healed for Life, the Lord spoke over me," Helen shared with a smile on her face. "God told me, 'You are beautiful, as beautiful as a rose... It's time to start seeing yourself that way.'"

The healing continued when Helen got home. Two days after the conference, God spoke to her again: "You are not a victim." The weeping started once more. She cried uncontrollably and God continued to speak. "You are my child. You are my child." The truth started to permeate her innermost being and she began to realize that she really was a child of God. "I always saw that ugly little girl in the dark," Helen shared. "Suddenly, I could see a lovely little girl in the light. It was amazing how much peace and joy flooded my soul. I stayed on my journey of restoration and attended many more Healed for Life events. God worked in me at every one."

For most of Helen's life, the mention of her dad's name terrified her. Even the thought of being in the same nation as him tormented her, so she completely avoided her homeland. It seems unthinkable that Helen could ever feel affection for the man who terrorized her for years. Yet the healing she experienced was so deep and so real that it changed everything. Helen summed it up like this: "Seeing his face and feeling no fear, no anger, and only love, was overwhelming. Joy filled my heart as I hugged my dad for the first time in 25 years." After a childhood torn apart by trauma, God restored Helen's heart, her marriage, her self-worth and her entire life. This precious lady is now a dedicated member of our ministry team and has the privilege of bringing healing to others.

Isaiah 40:4 promises, "Every valley shall be exalted and every mountain and hill brought low; the crooked places shall be made straight and the rough places smooth." Whatever bleak seasons you have gone through, the Lord is able to lead you out the other side. He wants to heal what is broken and make every rough place smooth. He is ready to restore each precious piece of your heart. You do not need to limp your way through life. You can be secure and strong.

NOT ALONE

Jesus endured cruelty throughout His life, but the way He was treated in the days leading up to His death must have been the worst of all. Mark 15:16-20 (AMPC) tells the story of how He was ridiculed among a big crowd of men: "Then the soldiers led Him away to the courtyard inside the palace, that is, the Praetorium, and they called the entire detachment of soldiers together. And they dressed Him in [a] purple [robe], and, weaving together a crown of thorns, they placed it on Him. And they began to salute Him, Hail (greetings, good health to You, long life to You), King of the Jews! And they struck His head with a staff made of a [bamboo-like] reed and spat on Him and kept bowing their knees in homage to Him. And when they had [finished] making sport of Him, they took the purple [robe] off of Him and put His own clothes on Him. And they led Him out [of the city] to crucify Him."

Just hours before Jesus suffered excruciating pain on the cross, He was used for public entertainment. Led to an area where crowds of soldiers were gathered, ringleaders made a sport of abusing and mocking Jesus. They stripped Him of His clothes for everyone to see, then dressed Him in their outfits. They slapped Him, spat on Him and got the whole crowd ridiculing His vulnerability. No animal should ever be treated the way those men behaved towards Jesus.

If you have been made to feel worthless by the actions of others, the Lord understands your pain. Maybe you were bullied at school, in college or the workplace. You might have been ridiculed or put down. Jesus voluntarily suffered public humiliation so that He could relieve you of your distress. One of the ways that the enemy tries to keep you bound is by making you afraid of facing humiliating memories. There are times when we seek medical help knowing that we will have to experience more pain before healing. When my daughter's face was cut to shreds in the cycling accident, doctors had to clean grit out of the wounds before they could stitch her up. Short term pain was necessary to make the way for lasting healing. It will be important to make the decision that you are willing to face buried memories so that you can be healed of any trauma.

Jesus was tortured by the authorities and falsely accused by religious leaders. In John 10:11-12, Jesus said: "I am the good shepherd. The good shepherd gives His life for the sheep. But a hireling, he who is not the shepherd, one who does not own the sheep, sees the wolf coming and leaves the sheep and flees; and the wolf catches the sheep and scatters them." Maybe you were wounded by people who should have offered you protection. Perhaps, like that wolf, someone abandoned you when you desperately needed their help. You could have been let down by leaders or authorities. You may find it tough to trust for fear of being betrayed again. God wants to heal your heart and renew your faith. Once you are restored, you will be able to trust again, safe in the knowledge that any time you are hurt, you can be healed.

WHEN DARTS FLY

Cutting words can tear us apart. Proverbs 12:18a says, "There is one who speaks like the piercings of a sword..." This scripture compares cruel remarks with a stabbing. Just as a knife attack can be fatal, verbal abuse can choke its victims. It's not just what is said, but the way that insults are hurled that can be crippling. If you have been attacked with words, please don't underestimate the damage that may have been caused. If you had been stabbed, you would rush to the emergency room. The enemy will probably tell you that it's easier to ignore emotional pain, but your future depends upon your emotional, as well as your physical, health.

Proverbs 4:23 is clear: your heart determines the course of your life. Buried pain will affect your reactions and decisions, whether you realize it or not. Unresolved trauma makes us avoid people or places. It causes us to hide when we should step up, or freeze when we should be fearless. Romans 8:14 tells us that that the sons and daughters of the living God should be directed by the Holy Spirit, not by unresolved emotional pain.

Verbal attacks come in many guises, including insults, ridicule, twisted truth, exposed secrets, bullying, and accusation. Each of these is cruel and can crush even a strong soul. There is something about bullying, whether it is experienced by a child or an adult, that is particularly vicious. Bullying is when someone who has some sort of perceived or actual weakness is antagonized by another who has a form of strength. The 'weakness' could be age, size, seniority, isolation or accent - the list is endless. Bullying is cowardly, it is cruel, and it can be mortifying. Bullying usually involves a mixture of harassment and humiliation which can strip its victims of any sense of dignity. It is often shocking, and it can make a person feel ashamed and exposed.

The Bible calls satan 'the accuser of the brethren' because accusation is one of the devil's most trusted tactics for damaging Christians. Accusation is a mix of judgement and vitriol, often laced with hatred. Full of blame, it can make its targets feel disqualified, and that can cause even a strong soul to throw in the towel.

GETTING PERSONAL

Some time ago, my husband Paul and I went through a distressing season. Serious accusations were leveled against my husband. The irony was that they were as far from the truth as you could get. I was raised in a tiny village in the north of England which was fairly isolated and therefore homogeneous. Paul, in contrast, was brought up in a diverse inner-city neighborhood. He had always been surrounded by people from different cultures and never distinguished between anyone on the basis of their skin color or culture.

My husband and I were pastoring the multicultural church that he had planted twenty-five years earlier. Paul had dedicated much of his life to international ministry and had preached in many African nations. So, when my husband was accused of both racism, and not being sufficiently anti-racist, it was shocking. Over a two-month period, he was tarnished by a series of slurs about his values, motives, and conduct. Critical conversations were going on behind our backs. Of course, as leaders we make mistakes and I know we made more than we realized during this period. Being at fault to some degree does not stop criticism from hurting.

During this season, the security of our home was called into question and it was this that tipped my husband into anxiety. Protecting his family has always been at the top of his priorities. Having been raised in a rough neighborhood, he has witnessed criminality and violence that I have only ever seen on television. As a result, he is more aware than most of what human beings are capable of doing when they are full of hatred. The intense pressure of this period caused my hero to have an emotional breakdown.

WHEN STRONG MEN BREAK

It is hard enough to see the weak fall apart. It is even more difficult to witness the strong break. No one has ever loved me like he has. No one has ever protected me the way that Paul does. I respect my husband more than anyone I have ever met. As a result, watching that incredible man fall apart in front of my eyes broke my heart. I was intimidated by others' comments and ripped to shreds by their impact on my husband.

After everything calmed down, I found myself suffering from anxiety. The slightest reminder of the season we had just left sent me into a spin. News items about prejudice, passing references in conversations or any reminders about the people involved would cause instant and intense emotional reactions. My stomach would knot up while my heart rate would increase. Controlled breathing only brought momentary relief. Unresolved trauma would spring to the surface and instantly steal my peace.

DEEP RECESSES OF THE SOUL

I tried rebuking the fear and casting off my cares about the future, but that was only part of the problem. Shock and pain were trapped in my soul. I realized that two events during that period had traumatized me. I could not get rid of the anxiety until the pain was healed. And I could not get rid of the pain until I went back to those memories. I got into God's presence and told my Heavenly Father how much it had hurt to see my husband break into pieces. As I prayed, I told the Lord how scared I was on the night when I could feel my husband's heart pounding out of the side of his chest. I told my Wonderful Counselor how tense and upsetting the home atmosphere was in that season.

It wasn't just the effect on my husband that hurt. Although my son was away, my beautiful daughter went through the whole trauma. She has a sensitive spirit and dislikes conflict. This period therefore took a toll on her. On several occasions, she broke down and wept as we talked. It made me so sad to see her being hurt just because she was our daughter. I poured all this pain out before the Lord in prayer and He healed my heart. After the healing flowed, I was able to deal with the spirit of intimidation. It wasn't long before I was back to full strength. Words that once triggered anxiety now passed by unnoticed. Faces that had caused concern now provoked compassion. The way we know that we have been healed is that the memories that once triggered negative reactions lose their power.

THE MARKS OF VIOLENCE

Perhaps you were brutally beaten during childhood under the guise of correction. Maybe you were assaulted as an adult by a stranger, or perhaps even by someone you knew. Enduring physical and emotional distress in the same moment can be devastating. You feel like you're being bombarded by fear, pain, shock and disbelief all at the same time. Too often in a situation like this, we shut down inside. The trauma can feel so intense that we disconnect ourselves in self-protection.

If you've done this, you may well look back at certain events without emotion. It might feel like you're looking at someone else's life. However, you probably contend with fear or anger. It may be that small things cause you to fly off the handle or perhaps you have a sense of dread in certain circumstances. God wants to take the rage and anxiety away, but your freedom may depend upon you being healed from the pain associated with the trauma. For that to happen, you usually need to reconnect emotionally with what happened to you. Start by giving the Lord access to every memory and experience of your life. When you get healed, overcoming anger, fear, and other negative emotions becomes easier.

JESUS HAS BEEN THERE

Jesus understands the pain of physical abuse. John 19:1 (TPT) says, "Then Pilate ordered Jesus to be brutally beaten with a whip of leather straps embedded with metal." The flesh on Jesus' back will have been ripped off as He was whipped - not just once or twice, but thirty-nine times. Jesus was a carpenter, so He must have been a strong man. However, the damage to His physical body was so immense that a man called Simon had to be asked to carry Jesus' cross the mile or so to Golgotha.

The executioners responsible for crucifying Jesus hammered nails straight through His wrists and His feet. He bled from His lacerated back, His hands, His feet, His side where He was stabbed and His grazed head. Isaiah 52:14 (AMPC) says, "[For many, the Servant of God became an object of horror; many were astonished at Him.] His face and His whole appearance were marred..." Your Lord understands how it feels to be brutalized. He suffered so that you could experience healing.

We will look at how our Savior heals, but first we need to understand an important issue. The enemy wants to exploit old pain and use it to cause additional damage. One way he does this is by trying to lock you up in an emotional prison. This can happen when traumatic memories get buried in your soul. You may deny the pain or try to avoid it because facing it seems too difficult. As a result, a part of your heart gets locked up. However, the Lord wants to shine His light into the hidden corners of your heart: "The spirit of a man is the lamp of the Lord, searching *all* the inner depths of his heart" (Proverbs 20:27). Just as a doctor treating a stab victim would carefully clean out the wound before dressing and bandaging the affected area, so God wants to reach into that place of pain and heal you where it hurts.

THE BALM OF GILEAD

The Old Testament speaks of a healing balm that was made in a place called Gilead in Israel. It was an expensive medicinal ointment with great healing properties. As a result of His death and resurrection, Jesus Himself becomes our Balm of Gilead. When we surrender our agony to Him and allow Him to tend to buried pain, His balm flows like liquid love into the hidden hurts in our hearts. As buried trauma is healed, freedom becomes possible.

Psalms 107:13-14 says, "Then they cried out to the Lord in their trouble, and He saved them out of their distresses. He brought them out of darkness and the shadow of death, and broke their chains in pieces." Healing leads to glorious freedom. Listen to verse 14 in the Message Translation: "He led you out of your dark, dark cell, broke open the jail and led you out." It goes on to say, "He shattered the heavy jailhouse doors, he snapped the prison bars like matchsticks!" (Psalms 107:16 MSG). Facing trauma can be difficult, but the restoration out the other side is magnificent.

The best-selling author and expert in human behavior, Jordan Petersen, made an extraordinary statement that went something like this: "Any memory that is older than eighteen months that still produces negative emotion needs addressing." I could not agree more. I encourage you to change your perspective on painful memories. Instead of thinking that it is acceptable to bury or ignore them, please see it as vital that you allow the Lord to heal any uncomfortable recollection.

SURROUNDED BY ANGER AND ARGUMENTS

Fiona's mom was heavily pregnant when the domestic violence hit an all-time high. "Night after night, I cried myself to sleep, desperate for it to stop," Fiona recalled. "The house was filled with anger, arguments, voices shrieking, and doors slamming. My dad hit my mom's pregnant belly. He hit her back, her face and anywhere he could. He hurled abuse at her and my unborn baby sister. It was terrifying. Then I had to watch mom cover up blemishes and bruises for months on end."

It was at the tender age of eight that Fiona made a vow that controlled her life decades later. With her fingers plugged in her ears to block out the screams and her eyes tightly shut, she determined, "I will never let a man treat me like that. I will never be weak." You may think to yourself that Fiona's promise to herself was sensible. Unfortunately, negative vows (especially those made whilst judging the actions of another person), are damaging for several reasons.

Numbers 30:2 says, "If a man... swears an oath to bind himself by some agreement, he shall not break his word; he shall do according to all that proceeds out of his mouth." Vows bind our hearts and our behavior. When we make a vow, we take our lives into our own hands. Proverbs 28:26 tell us that, "He who trusts in his own heart is a fool..." Our vows are usually an attempt to protect ourselves, but only the Lord God is capable of that. If I vow that I will never be weak, then I will be compelled to be strong in my own strength. I will be forced to keep others at arm's length and to build walls around my heart or life.

POURING OUT PAIN IN PRAYER

Fiona attended one of our events, Fixing the Foundations, where we deal with the five foundational relationships: mothers, fathers, peers, leaders and romance. We minister into what went wrong, but also into what never went right. During the session about mothers, the Holy Spirit took Fiona back to that traumatic period in her life. She poured out her pain in prayer as the Lord healed her precious heart. She felt a lightness she had never known before. Later in the day, when we ministered on romance, the Lord revealed how the vows that Fiona had made as a child had affected her entire married life.

"Right from the start, I was a controlling, bossy wife," Fiona explained. "I always insisted on leading in the home. Although I knew that the Bible taught that the husband should be the head of the home, I saw submission as weakness, so I resisted. I could not stand the thought of my husband being boss in any context whatsoever. I was bound by my need to lead. When I broke the vows that I made more than twenty years earlier, it was like unlocking a prison door. What I had intended for my self-protection had instead kept me bound. I left that event feeling free: free to love, free to submit, and even free to lead. It is now more than a year since that healing encounter, and I am still enjoying the benefits. Not only in my marriage, but in many of my relationships."

Violence dates back to the beginning. Adam and Eve suffered the unimaginable pain of seeing their son Cain murder their other son

Abel. They must have been shocked and grief-stricken to lose two children in one day. Although Cain lived, he was banished. King David experienced similar sadness when his son Absalom killed his half-brother Amnon. Many others have experienced terrible cruelty and come out the other side. Please don't bury pain any longer. Ask the Lord to heal you.

Isaiah 40:1-2 says, '"Comfort, yes, comfort My people!" Says your God. "Speak comfort to Jerusalem, and cry out to her, that her warfare is ended..."' Trauma is like living during wartime. Fear is all around; life is lived on a knife's edge and nerves are frayed. Although your circumstances may change, until trauma is healed it can still adversely affect your life. You may be fortunate enough to go for months or even years thinking all is well. Then a reminder causes an outburst or a shutdown. When you make a decision to let the Lord heal every part of your heart, you will begin an incredible journey to lasting peace and contentment. Before we pray, use the Trauma Tracker on the next page to help identify any hidden trauma.

CRUELTY TRAUMA TRACKER

Use the list below to identify any traumatic events you have experienced or witnessed. Put a check mark beside each category that is relevant to you and then write one adjective beside the event that best describes how you feel when you think about that experience. Ask the Holy Spirit to help you to complete the checklist.

☐ Abuse _____

☐ Abandonment _____

☐ Accusation _____

☐ Assault _____

☐ Attack _____

☐ Betrayal _____

☐ Bullying _____

☐ Fights _____

☐ Humiliation _____

☐ Mugging _____

☐ Rage _____

☐ Rape _____

☐ Ridicule _____

☐ Riots _____

☐ Torture   _____

☐ Verbal attack   _____

☐ Violence   _____

☐ War   _____

☐ Other   _____

Take note of any negative emotions that are stirred up as a result of thinking back to old experiences. Discomfort, anger, regret, sadness, disquiet or any other negative reaction is an indication that you still need to be healed. In Chapter Eight, you will be able to come back to this list as an aid to your healing. I would love to lead you in prayer:

Heavenly Father,

I am willing to face the pain of trauma that is buried in my heart. I ask You to shine Your light deep down and reveal any hidden hurts. I ask You to gently uncover any wounds that I have denied, ignored, or buried. I don't want fear or pain to control any area of my life or my relationships any longer.

If I have detached myself emotionally from my pain, I ask for Your help, Lord. Please would you reconnect me with my emotions so that I can feel again? I understand that You made me in Your image with the ability to feel pain. I ask You to restore my soul - my mind, my will, and my emotions - to its original purpose. Reveal the moments that I pushed pain down or disconnected myself and heal me, I pray, Oh Lord.

My heart is open to You, Jesus. Please take me on a journey to wholeness so that I can be free to fulfill my purpose.

In Jesus' name, I pray,

Amen.

As the Lord reveals hidden pain or brings you back to long-forgotten memories, talk to Him about the experience. Tell Him what happened and ask Him to heal your heart. We will go into more detail about how to be healed of trauma wounds in section three.

Chapter 4

LOSS

Pacing up and down the hospital corridor, I just kept worshiping. I knew that God was my healer, so I believed that praise was my best weapon. While the crash team were still working on our little girl, my husband rushed through the doors. Directed to the side room where doctors were trying to revive Naomi, my husband fell to his knees at the foot of her bed, held our baby girl's toes in his hands, and cried aloud, "She will live and not die!" Moments later, our daughter's heart began to beat again. It was still touch and go, but what a confirmation that the Lord had Naomi's life in His hands. It was about midnight.

Not long after our first miracle, Naomi had another cardiac arrest. The team began to resuscitate her again. For a second time, our awesome God came through. Test results showed that our daughter had serious septicemia (an infection in her blood that was attacking her organs), so a specialist team from a major London hospital was called. When they arrived at around 4am, it felt like knights in shining armor had just walked through the door. Hope sprang up in my heart as they set to work on our two-year old's tiny frame.

It was a few hours later when Naomi suffered her third and final cardiac arrest. By this time, there was a huge team working together to save our princess's life. She was wrapped in a silver foil blanket, wore a foil cap on her head and had wires coming out of every conceivable place. The team surrounded her as they attempted resuscitation. Then, one by one, medics started to leave until there were only two or three doctors remaining. The consultant in charge turned to my husband and said, "We usually attempt to resuscitate a child for ten minutes. With an adult, we will continue for twenty-five minutes. We have been doing CPR on your daughter now for nearly half an hour." Our only child had died.

THE END OF THE WORLD AS WE KNEW IT

We drove back from the hospital in a daze. Naomi's car seat was strapped in its usual place behind me and her dolly lay next to it. My husband and I said nothing during the twenty-minute journey home. We walked through the front door completely devastated. There are two telephone calls that stand out the most. When I rang my father, I asked him if he was sitting down. In shock, he blurted out, "She's not dead, is she?" Another conversation that I will never forget was with my co-worker. Our children had played together many times. As I shared our heartbreak, she dropped her phone and fell to the ground in shock. Naomi had only been sick for a few days, so nothing could have possibly prepared us (or any of our loved ones) for this terrible tragedy. Our life as we knew it was over forever.

If you had told me back then that I could ever recover from such agonizing loss, I would have thought that you were out of your mind. And yet, over the weeks and months that followed, our loving Heavenly Father did what I thought could not be done. Jesus healed our shattered hearts, one broken piece at a time. Through a mixture of supernatural healing encounters and an instinctive refusal to push pain down, the Lord restored us from the inside out. I did what David did in Psalms 118:5: "I called on the Lord in distress; the Lord answered me and set me in a broad place." I am going to share more about how we can be healed in section three, but for now I want you to allow hope to start to arise on the inside, because God is faithful, and He is able.

TORN APART

In the midst of a fierce civil war, a child lost both his dad and his grandfather at the same time. 2 Samuel 4:4 (AMPC) tells the story: "Jonathan, Saul's son, had a son who was a cripple in his feet. He was five years old when the news came out of Jezreel [of the deaths] of Saul and Jonathan... His name was Mephibosheth." In one tragic day, a child's world was torn apart. In chapter two, we focused on this little boy's terrible injuries. Now we are going to look at the impact of sudden loss.

God's plan was that every child would be nurtured by both their father and their mother. Proverbs 4:3 (AMPC) reveals the Lord's intention for parenting: "When I [Solomon] was a son with my father [David], tender and the only son in the sight of my mother [Bathsheba]." Solomon felt the love and care of both of his parents. In the same way, the Lord wanted you to enjoy the unconditional love of your father and your mother. When a child grows up knowing that they are treasured - not for succeeding, but just for being themselves - it creates a wonderful sense of stability. The role of parents is to raise secure children who can become confident and independent adults.

THE VACUUM

If you don't remember your dad putting his arm around your shoulder with warmth and affection, then God wants to heal you heart. If you never felt cherished by your mother, then it probably created a vacuum that the Lord wants to fill. You may have missed out as a result of death or divorce. Maybe you never knew your mother or father, or perhaps your parents were so ill, absent, broken or dysfunctional that they couldn't give what you needed. Whatever the reason, if you were denied the lavish love from your father, your mother or even both parents, it will probably have affected your view of your own value.

I encourage you to ask the Lord to heal you from the inside out. Your worth is not determined by what you do. Your value is not measured by what you add to the lives of others. An absence of unconditional parental affirmation can cause you to struggle with those concepts. My book 'My Whole Heart' will help you on your journey. The Lord created family and modelled unconditional love because He knew that it was the key to inner peace and security. The Lord wanted a happy family life for Mephibosheth, and He wanted that for you too.

REELING WITH SHOCK

Instead, this tiny boy went through the trauma of his dad's sudden death. One day, his father was strong and well. The next, he was gone. His entire world crashed. Shock is horrible. It winds its victims like a punch in the guts. It is defined as a sudden, violent disturbance. Trauma almost always incorporates shock, but the point I would like you to grasp is that shock alone is traumatic. It is alarming, confusing and distressing. We are habit-seeking creatures who thrive on consistency and schedules. Sudden disturbances can open the door to all sorts of fears.

King Nebuchadnezzar of Babylon experienced a terrible shock. The account in Daniel 5:6 (AMPC) is a powerful depiction of how hard it can hit: "Then the color and the... brightness of the king's face was changed, and his [terrifying] thoughts troubled and alarmed him; the joints and muscles of his hips and back gave way and his knees smote together." It takes a toll, both emotionally and physically. It hits our sleep, appetite, digestive system, blood pressure and more. Recovery after shock is vital.

If you went through major disruption in childhood, you may still bear the marks in adult life. Sometimes shock leaves behind inexplicable anxiety or a dislike of change. It may make you oversensitive to certain sights or sounds. We will discover how you can be free from fear later in this book. For now, I encourage you to stop for a moment. Ask the Holy Spirit to reveal any of your reactions or behavior that might be rooted in past distress.

THE GAPING HOLE

To experience such loss at such a tender age must have been overwhelming. Mephibosheth probably didn't understand what had happened and no doubt kept wondering when his dad would come home. From everything that we know about his father Jonathan, he was a kind and considerate man. For many little boys, their dad is their hero. If that was the kind of relationship that Mephibosheth had with his father, then the sense of loss will have been devastating. A good father makes his children feel both special and safe. When he leaves or dies, there is a gaping hole in that child's life.

If you are feeling that painful absence as you read, the Lord wants you to know that He longs to heal your heart. It was never God's plan that you would suffer. He only ever wanted good for your life because you are His child (see James 1:17). It hurts Him to see you in pain. Psalms 34:18 (TPT) says, "The Lord is close to all whose hearts are crushed by pain..." Your Heavenly Father is with you right now, ready to restore what is broken in your heart. He understands your disappointment, but if you will let Him heal, He will start a new work in your life.

The pain of loss catches up with us all at one time or another. If you haven't yet lost someone you love, then unfortunately, you probably will. If you have, then you know the depth of sadness that death can leave behind. The ache is intense, and it is physical. When my husband and I lost our two-year-old daughter, my heart was plunged to unwanted depths and I hurt in places I didn't know existed. A parent who lost his teenage daughter to suicide described the pain like this: "My insides are being ripped apart, twenty-four seven."

We will deal with the immense power of pain in chapter six, but I want you to know now that there is no agony that God cannot heal. Psalms 33:15 says, "He fashions their hearts individually..." The Lord made your soul as unique as your fingerprint. He sculpted your heart, and He knows how to put it back together, even after it has been shattered into a thousand pieces. Psalms 147:3 (AMPC) reassures us that, "He heals the brokenhearted and binds up their wounds [curing their pains and their sorrows]." This scripture does *not* say that time heals. Time does not possess that power. It says that our loving Heavenly Father can cure all our pain and sorrow.

CHANGED FOREVERMORE

Mephibosheth lost his father, his grandfather and his future. His life changed forever on that fateful day. He went from being a member of the royal family to an enemy of the state. His grandfather, Israel's King Saul, was at war with Judah's King David. Soon after Saul and Jonathan died, David was crowned king over all Israel and the family of the previous administration will have been viewed as rivals. Of course, five-year-old Mephibosheth will not have known that, but children are very sensitive to atmosphere. I'm certain he will have felt the stark change. He won't have known why everything was suddenly so different, and probably so scary.

Maybe you were uprooted in childhood and moved to another neighborhood, or even another nation. You may have lost friends, family and familiar surroundings. Perhaps you didn't understand your new culture or maybe you didn't know the local language. People all around you may have been telling you how grateful you should be for your new home, but perhaps you felt lonely, scared and different. When we are under pressure to be thankful, sometimes we feel unable to grieve what we have lost. Guilt about our true feelings can make us bury the pain deep inside.

You may have had your security stolen after a robbery at home or a mugging. Perhaps you once enjoyed a wonderful sense of protection until one incident that left you feeling vulnerable and shaken. When someone violates your 'safe place', it can have a devastating impact. Isaiah 61:8 (NLT) says, "For I, the Lord, love justice. I hate robbery and wrongdoing. I will faithfully reward my people for their suffering..." God understands the impact that an attack can have, and He is ready to restore. Perhaps your loss wasn't the result of criminality, but financial ruin. Maybe you lost your job, your livelihood or even your home.

DEALING WITH DISTRESS

Before Mephibosheth was born, David went through a terrible experience. After impressing King Saul with his harp playing and giant-slaying, he was invited to live at the palace. The young warrior loved his time in the royal household. However, David suddenly fell from favor. That alone must have been difficult. When you suddenly discover that you have become the enemy, it is devastating. Not only did David lose a vital relationship with his spiritual father, but he also lost his job and his home.

King Saul turned on David. Despite his unswerving loyalty, David became the target of Saul's army who were instructed to find him and kill him. The young warrior was forced to run for his life. He had no option other than living rough. It was during these terrible times that David learned to pour out his pain in prayer. In Psalms 25:16-17 (AMPC) he cried to God: "[Lord] turn to me and be gracious to me, for I am lonely and afflicted. The troubles of my heart are multiplied; bring me out of my distresses." Listen to the emotional detail in David's prayer: he told the Lord that he felt lonely, in pain and grieved (that's what afflicted means). This strong, soon-to-be-king explained that his heart was troubled and that he felt terribly distressed. He shared his deepest feelings with God.

All too often, our prayers are professional. We speak to the Lord using detached, spiritual language. We talk to Him the way we might speak to a boss, or a distant relative. Please do not be guarded with God. He wants you to treat Him like a close, loving father. He knows every detail of your heart and life anyway, but He loves to hear from you, His child. And when you share your true feelings with your Heavenly Father, not only will you experience relief and healing. You will also feel close to Him.

DAVID'S DARKEST HOUR

After a decade of living in exile, things started to look up for David. A growing group of men joined the warrior. They started to enjoy some success and stability. They were given a city called Ziklag by the Philistines which was beginning to feel like home. However, on returning from a failed attempt in battle one day, they saw their city in the distance. It had burned to the ground. 1 Samuel 30:3-4 (AMPC) describes their first reactions: "So David and his men came to the town, and behold, it was burned, and their wives and sons and daughters were taken captive. Then David and the men with him lifted up their voices and wept until they had no more strength to weep."

These men lost absolutely everything. Their city was destroyed, their homes were burned, and their families were missing. They had no idea at that point if they would ever see their loved ones again. People often preach about this terrible tragedy, focusing on the last part of verse six which says that David strengthened himself in the Lord. However, before David ever attempted to build himself up, he broke down before the Lord. Together with his men, he wept until he had no more tears left. It is better to become strong when we have first surrendered our pain.

In times of tragedy, it is important to offload your pain in God's presence. If you have suffered trauma, but have struggled to cry before the Lord, please take time right now to ask the Holy Spirit to help you to share your heart with Him in prayer. A precious lady who lost both her parents in quick succession told me about the grief counselling she received: "I talked and cried, and then talked and cried some more. That's what counselling is all about, isn't it?" I thank God for anointed therapists who can help their clients to connect with complex, hidden issues. In the same way, if you can learn to share your deepest concerns and greatest pains with God in prayer, then I think you will be learning what it means to know the Lord as your Wonderful Counsellor.

HOSPITAL HORROR

Let's go back to the story I shared at the start of this book. Veronica was working in a central London hospital when the lethal COVID 19 pandemic spread like wildfire across the British capital. Wards started to fill up as seriously ill men and women occupied hospital beds. Staff were covered from head to toe in protective clothing in an attempt to keep the deadly virus away. Although the gloves, visors and overalls were vital for staff safety, the sight was almost apocalyptic and quite frightening. Veronica was looking after patients who were fighting for every breath. Ventilators whirred, alarms sounded, and thudding footsteps hurried towards critically sick people. What made things even worse was watching patients arrive sick, then stabilizing, before suddenly getting much worse. Death was a daily event. This normally calm London hospital looked like something out of a horror movie.

Working long shifts, often without breaks, Veronica would come home only to shower, sleep, and then return to the frontline. It wasn't long before the trauma of this war against sickness took its toll. Veronica explained, "I was living on a knife edge. Stressed, stretched and afraid of making even the tiniest mistake, I became completely overwhelmed. I was irritable during the little time that I had at home, which affected my family too. I struggled to sleep."

IT'S REAL

If you have seen terrible sights or heard disturbing events, please don't underestimate the impact that they might have had on you.

Maybe you saw things as a child that shocked your spirit and the buried images still make you recoil. Perhaps you witnessed devastation and terrible pictures have been branded on your memory. Listen to how the Bible describes the distress of seeing dreadful things: "Therefore my loins are filled with pain; pangs have taken hold of me, like the pangs of a woman in labor. I was distressed when I heard it; I was dismayed when I saw it. My heart wavered; fearfulness frightened me..." (Isaiah 21:3-4). Trauma can grip its victims, even if they weren't directly affected.

Veronica was a member of Harvest, our church in London, so I ministered to her one evening by telephone. She was traumatized by the horror that she was witnessing daily. I helped her to pour out the shock, sadness and strain of the ward in prayer before the Lord. She cried, she sighed, then she laid it all down at the feet of Jesus. This precious lady told God that she felt traumatized and overwhelmed by all the suffering. She shared that she had had enough of it all. Afterwards, I prayed for our Heavenly Father to fill her afresh with His wonderful love. The stress washed off Veronica and her peace was restored. Perhaps more importantly, she developed a prayer habit of offloading the strain of her shift on the Lord each day as soon as she arrived home from work.

UNTOLD AGONY

One of history's great tragedies happened at the time of the birth of Jesus. Matthew 2:16 (NLT) tells the story: "Herod was furious when he realized that the wise men had outwitted him. He sent soldiers to kill all the boys in and around Bethlehem who were two years old and under." I have no idea how many boys were murdered, but historians put the number of deaths at somewhere between 60,000 and 140,000 babies. Thousands upon thousands of families were plunged into terrible grief as a result of the jealousy of one cruel leader.

Sometimes, our suffering is drawn out longer than it needs to be because we feel unable to receive the healing that our Heavenly

Father is offering. Matthew 2:17b-18 (NLT) continues: 'Herod's brutal action fulfilled what God had spoken through the prophet Jeremiah: "A cry was heard in Ramah—weeping and great mourning. Rachel weeps for her children, refusing to be comforted, for they are dead."' In this account, a grieving mother called Rachel could not be comforted. The reason for her prolonged distress is spelled out clearly. Something on the inside of Rachel was resisting restoration. She could not get her head or her heart around the devastating reality that she would never see her little boy again.

Most translations express Matthew 2:18 slightly differently: "Rachel weeping for her children, refusing to be comforted, because they are no more." The finality of her tragedy made her feel unable to accept comfort. She refused to be consoled, probably because she did not want to be healed if she could not have her baby back. Many times, agony can have that effect on its victims. What has happened is wrong, so even the idea of being healed can seem distasteful. How could a mother really recover after losing the child she carried in her womb for nine months? How could a father heal after losing his own flesh and blood?

To suggest that they could be truly happy again would surely undermine the depth of the love that they had for their child. The same emotional logic can be applied to many other examples of tragic loss. A husband whose wife died in her prime, leaving him and their children behind, may balk at the idea of healing. A twin who is suddenly separated from the one with whom they shared almost every waking moment may refuse to accept that they could ever enjoy life alone.

However, there is no distress that God cannot heal. There is no pain that He cannot take away. Even when we do not understand *why* we had to suffer, He will mend our broken hearts if we surrender. The route to restoration almost always involves a journey of many healing experiences, rather than a one-time encounter. However, we can be completely free of pain. Psalms

147:3 (AMPC) says, "He heals the brokenhearted and binds up their wounds [curing their pains and their sorrows]."

RUNNNG FOR HELP

I am certain that if Rachel (in Matthew 2) had run into the arms of her Heavenly Father and asked Him to heal every corner of her heart, then she would have been restored. When we let go of every question, every reason why it should not have happened, and when we give up our right to justice and instead surrender every sadness to God, He *will* heal our hearts. I can't tell you why some people die, and others get healed. I know it feels desperately unfair. What I do know is that God is kind, and He is longing to take your pain away. In section two, we will look in more detail at some of the barriers to restoration. We will return to Rachel's story which is told in the book of Matthew.

I remember the day that I told the Lord, "I would rather have my daughter back from the dead. But if I can't have her, I ask You for the next best thing: will You heal my heart, Lord?" I made a choice to chase my healing. I decided that I would pursue a new life, even though it wasn't the version of life that I had wanted. We used to sing a song in our church that went something like: "I have a living hope, I have a future, God has a plan for me, of this I'm sure, of this I'm sure..." Many times, I sang this song to declare my faith in God to turn our lives around. I decided to embrace life - even though it felt so painful - and to pursue healing.

WHAT HAVE YOU LOST?

Maybe you lost your marriage. After years of waiting for the right one, you eventually met your mate and married. Perhaps you heard clearly from the Lord that this was the person for you. Then, despite giving your best, your spouse was never satisfied and instead chased after other people. Discovering that the love of your life has been unfaithful is both shocking and devastating. Your trust is shattered, your truth is found to be a lie and there is the sense of humiliation. Referring to adultery, Proverbs 5:9 (TPT) says, "In disgrace you will relinquish your honor to another, and all your remaining years will be squandered - given over to the cruel one." Unfaithfulness brings dishonor to both husband and wife, irrespective of who was at fault. Afterwards, the enemy wants to keep you in a prison of pain. He wants to mark you forever with betrayal and devastation. I want you to know that however hard it may seem to believe it, the Lord is able to heal your shattered heart and bring wholeness.

Maybe you have encountered devastation in every direction. You have lost loved ones, your livelihood, your security, even trusted relationships. The prophet Jeremiah 4:20 (AMPC) experienced pain like that: "News of one violent disaster and calamity comes close after another, for the whole land is laid waste; suddenly are my tents... destroyed..." He described how the shock of devastation made him feel: "... I writhe in pain! Oh, the walls of my heart! My heart is disquieted and throbs aloud within me; I cannot be silent!" (Jeremiah 4:19b AMPC). In agony, the so-called weeping prophet poured out his heart like water before the face of the Lord (see Lamentations 2:19). No matter what you have gone through, if you will do the same, you will start to find relief. Before we pray, please use the Trauma Tracker on the next page to help identify any hidden pain.

LOSS TRAUMA TRACKER

Use the list below to identify any traumatic events you have experienced or witnessed. Put a check mark beside each category that is relevant to you and then write one adjective beside the event that best describes how you feel when you think about that experience. Ask the Holy Spirit to help you to complete the checklist.

☐ Childhood _____

☐ Community _____

☐ Death _____

☐ Dignity _____

☐ Familiarity _____

☐ Family _____

☐ Fiance _____

☐ Friends _____

☐ Home _____

☐ Innocence _____

☐ Job _____

☐ Livelihood _____

☐ Marriage _____

☐ Miscarriage _____

☐ Nation   _____

☐ Possessions   _____

☐ Security   _____

☐ Other   _____

Take note of any negative emotions that are stirred up as a result of thinking back to old experiences. Discomfort, anger, regret, sadness, disquiet or any other negative reaction is an indication that you still need to be healed. In Chapter Eight, you will be able to come back to this list as an aid to your healing. I would love to lead you in prayer:

Heavenly Father,

I have been hurt by loss (*tell the Lord how you have been affected in as much detail as possible*). I have carried pain and dreadful memories buried in my heart. I ask You to shine Your light into my soul and reveal unhealed wounds. Where I have not dealt properly with what happened, I ask You to bring the hurt to the surface. Where I have buried pain, I ask You to bring old wounds to my remembrance so that I can be healed. I ask You to expose any forgotten trauma that is hindering my life so that I can be free to fulfill my purpose.

Where I have witnessed death or loss that has branded my memory, I ask You to lead me to healing (*now tell the Lord what you saw and how it made you feel. Explain what was most distressing to God.*) I want my heart to be free of weight and pain, so I ask You to do a deep work within.

Have Your way in every area of my heart and life.

In Jesus' name, I pray,

Amen.

TEN TRAUMAS

Before you move to the next section, take some time to prayerfully review your Trauma Trackers. Ask the Holy Spirit to help you identify up to ten traumatic events or experiences that still affect you in one way or another. The events may be related. For example, a diagnosis and a harrowing medical procedure may have taken place on the same day, but they are separate events. Give this some prayerful thought. When you are ready, note them below. We will come back to these at the end of chapter eight.

1) _____

2) _____

3) _____

4) _____

5) _____

6) _____

7) _____

8) _____

9) _____

10) _____

Surrender these experiences to the Lord, one by one, and ask Him to prepare your heart for lasting healing.

CONSEQUENCES

Trauma altars lives. Folk who were once calm and collected become agitated and restless. People who were confident become unsure of themselves and those who once enjoyed rewarding relationships struggle to trust. In this section, we are going to expose the devastating effects of trauma so that we can start to bring healing and freedom.

Chapter 5

FEAR

The terror of the crash, the alarm of that brutal attack or the horror of that hospital ward. Trauma is frightening. Often the dread that it leaves behind is as bad, if not worse, than the emotional pain. Your sleep may have been disturbed, you might be afraid of certain places or your confidence may have been severely knocked. Even mild trauma can leave a trail of intimidation. You could lie at wake at night worrying about a presentation or a medical appointment because you fear a repeat of a distressing experience.

Right upfront, I want to remind you that fear is your enemy. Fear involves torment (1 John 4:18), which is defined as *severe mental distress*. You may struggle with dread as a result of a terrible attack years ago. You might have faced humiliation that knocked you for six. If you churn inside, feel sick to your stomach, get plagued by your own thoughts, or lie awake worrying, God wants to set you free from the torment. Even if the dread is occasional - for example, you're fine until you're in a car or at the doctor's - Jesus paid the price to give you the victory over all fear.

Torment is one reason why fear is foul. The second is that it seeks to control your life. Proverbs 29:25 (TPT) says, "Fear and intimidation is a trap that holds you back." When you are trapped, you are unable to move. The devil wants to keep you constrained. He wants to hold back your progress and keep you from fulfilling your destiny. The spirit of fear taunts you and tells lies to prevent you from stepping out. It makes you wary of people, places and even of God's plans. In this chapter, we will expose different types of fear. Awareness is the first step to freedom.

SPINNING

When I woke up on the days immediately after our daughter died, I would sometimes forget the loss for a few moments. The thing that usually reminded me of her death was the empty space in the corner of our bedroom where her baby listening monitor used to sit. Somehow that sight had the power to send me into a terrible spin.

I would see my little girl lying unwell on my tummy in the middle of the night, then I would remember my fear as she kept snuggling as close as she could. I would find myself back in that horrible place of panic and despair, not knowing what to do. Soon, I would see her asleep the following morning as I went to work. I would watch myself leave the house (wishing I had stayed). Next, I would be on the train to London and I would hear that mobile phone call with my husband and the angst in our voices.

Finally, I would receive that message. Naomi had been rushed to hospital in an ambulance and I must leave work immediately. I would see the corner of the meeting room where I was standing as I listened to that fateful voicemail. I got to the hospital as quickly as possible, but the rest is history. Once or twice, the memories sucked me into such deep dread that I momentarily lost my grip on reality.

THE POWER OF FLASHBACKS

A flashback is a vivid recollection of a traumatic event. Certain experiences, situations or people may trigger flashbacks. These might include reminders of the trauma, such as particular smells, certain sounds, or specific places. The screeching of brakes or the whirring of sirens might take you straight back to that terrible accident. The mention of certain people, a type of disease or specific locations could pull you into a downward spiral. You may find things difficult on significant dates, such as the anniversary of a traumatic experience or a loved one's birthday. Alternatively, there may be words that act as triggers - or even books, movies and songs.

Flashbacks are distressing so the temptation is to hide from the rewind. Our memories end up becoming objects of dread and develop a power of their own to cause anguish. As a result, we shut away certain episodes in 'no-go' rooms hidden in our hearts. We dare not open the doors of those rooms because the contents are too painful. When something opens the door, we try to turn our faces away so that we don't have to witness the sight, feel the pain or experience the shame again. We think that by avoiding those recollections, we are helping ourselves to recover. The truth is that if you run away from distressing memories, they gain power through your fear.

Whenever we have suffered any type of trauma, fear will try to worm its way into our lives. However, it is an enemy so we must refuse to listen to its instructions. Fear tells us who or what to avoid, what to say and how to think. Please don't give in. It may take time to conquer, but your freedom is worth the fight. Psalms 23:4 (TPT) says, "Lord, even when your path takes me through the valley of deepest darkness, fear will never conquer me, for you already have! You remain close to me and lead me through it all the way. Your authority is my strength and my peace. The comfort of Your love takes away my fear. I'll never be lonely, for You are near." Decide right now that you won't allow fear to control any area of your life any longer.

PANIC ATTACKS

A panic attack is an intense assault of anxiety which is characterized by feelings of doom. Your heart pounds, you can't breathe, and you may feel like you're dying or going crazy. Panic attacks often strike without any warning, and sometimes with no obvious trigger. You may have had one panic attack, or you could have experienced recurring episodes. Because the attack itself is so distressing, the fear of having another panic attack can add to the problem. They are often brought on by specific situations, such as crossing a bridge, speeding in a car, or seeing a certain person. Alternatively, they can be triggered by a sudden, overwhelming dose of truth, such as the realization that a loved one is never coming back, or that a marriage really is over.

Jeremiah experienced terrible distress that affected his heart as well as his physical body. He described the trauma of seeing devastation all around him in Lamentations 1:20 (AMPC): "Behold, O Lord, how distressed I am! My vital parts (emotions) are in tumult and are deeply disturbed; my heart cannot rest and is violently agitated within me... Outside the house the sword bereaves, at home there is [famine, pestilence] death!" His heart thumped in his chest and he felt terrible stress. The damaging effects of trauma are as old as trauma itself.

My first return to the office was about three weeks after our daughter died. I visited during a busy working day to see colleagues before my official return to work a week later. I wandered around my department chatting to one or two friends before reaching my desk. Something about seeing my desk brought me back to my tragedy. The last time I sat in that chair and looked out of that window, my little girl was alive. My heart pounded in my chest and I struggled to catch my breath as anxiety gripped me. I became completely overwhelmed and unable to cope with the intensity. One of my co-workers led me out of the open plan office and sat me down. After several minutes, the panic subsided.

THE WAY OUT

I met a doctor who ran a training session for leaders about ministering to people who suffer from panic attacks. I remember silently weeping my way through the workshop. I learned an important lesson that day. While we run away from painful memories, we stay bound by the fear of those events. If you get flashbacks or panic attacks, I encourage you to face the inner pictures that have tormented you. If you regularly turn away from certain memories, please rethink your reactions.

Fear's power is fear. The Bible puts it this way: "...fear involves torment..." (1 John 4:18). Let me explain. When we are afraid of particular memories, it is fear itself that makes those thoughts frightening. When we eliminate fear, we can look at the pictures that once tormented us and get healed of the hurt instead. The pain goes away, and those memories lose their sting.

The next time someone or something opens the door to that room in your heart, don't run away. Instead, invite the Holy Spirit to come in and ask Jesus to heal you of the pain of that memory. Look at the pictures of your past in your mind. Examine the memories that try to overwhelm you. Tell the Lord how much they hurt and why. As you face the flashbacks and share your distress with the Lord, the fear of those sights will diminish.

After that workshop by the Christian doctor, I brought every painful memory to Jesus. I asked Him to heal my heart, piece by piece. I told Him I would never again be afraid of facing difficult experiences. From that moment onwards, I brought every picture to Him when it came to mind. I was never again sucked into a downward spiral of flashbacks and I never again had a panic attack. I was not yet whole, but I was getting healed.

I DON'T WANT TO GO BACK THERE AGAIN

There is another type of fear. It is the dread of experiencing the same sort of pain again. This fear is more subtle and feels threatening. Anything that reminds you of the circumstances that led to the trauma may make you churn inside. Hearing about people suffering with certain symptoms may lead to undue stress. Seeing the school number flash up on your phone may cause panic. Even certain names or words might cause anxiety because you cannot stand the thought of history repeating itself.

The enemy wants you to be afraid of further hurt. He wants you to live in dread of it happening again. But the devil is a liar and most fear is based on his groundless threats. Proverbs 1:33 (NLT) says: "But all who listen to me will live in peace, untroubled by fear of harm." Fear is believing what the enemy says, while faith is believing what God says. When you are recovering from trauma, you need to be acutely aware of who has your attention.

After my husband and I went through a terribly difficult season, hearing certain words on the news or even in conversation felt like a punch in the guts. They would take me straight back to the storm. Like Lamentations 3:20 says, "My soul still remembers and sinks within me." If certain reminders cause you to crumple, it is important to acknowledge that you need to be set free. Don't avoid being exposed to those reminders. Instead, ask the Lord to deal with the root.

Talking it through with a friend afterwards, I explained that the season had felt like being beaten repeatedly. After I had been healed of the emotional cuts and bruises, I realized that I was still afraid of certain people. There was one person who made me shudder. Any communication from her made me nervous. I did not want to be judged or misunderstood anymore. I could not bear the thought of being attacked one more time.

ATTACKED

David suffered many betrayals and accusations. In Psalms 55:2-5 (AMPC), he cried out to the Lord after a lifelong friend stabbed him in the back: "...I am restless and distraught in my complaint...

[And I am distracted] at the noise of the enemy, because of the oppression and threats of the wicked; for they would cast trouble upon me, and in wrath they persecute me. My heart is grievously pained within me... Fear and trembling have come upon me; horror and fright have overwhelmed me." David described the fear and pain that he felt during this season of his life. He told the Lord how he felt when he was betrayed by his former friend.

Remember that our struggle is never against flesh and blood (see Ephesians 6:12). The devil is our enemy and demons are wicked. We must remember that people are not our real problem. This passage describes the effect that verbal attacks can have. Every word is troubling. They cause pain and often leave us trembling. Listen to the same passage in the New Living Translation: "I am overwhelmed by my troubles. My enemies shout at me, making loud and wicked threats. They bring trouble on me and angrily hunt me down. My heart pounds in my chest." (Psalms 55:2-4). This describes the state of someone who is gripped with fear, and not just pain.

If you have suffered any type of attack - verbal, physical, or sexual - it is vital that you ask the Lord to deal with the aftermath of fear. There is always the temptation to avoid anything that stirs up anxiety, but it is far better to evict every form of fear. It does require bravery to face the things that make you afraid, but the relief afterwards is well worth the temporary difficulty.

THE POWER OF WORDS

We are made in the image of God, so our words are powerful. They can bring life, yet they can also severely wound others. Proverbs 12:18 says, "There is one who speaks like the piercings of a sword..." Just as someone who has experienced a physical attack may struggle with fear afterwards, so you may be in shock after verbal assaults.

Some time ago, a long letter about me and my husband was circulated to several people. Half detailed my mistakes and inadequacies, and the other half listed grievances against my husband. When the letter arrived, I was in an important ministry team meeting. The letter was dropped on my desk and I saw the name of the sender. Instinctively, I knew it was a character attack and felt an instant thump to the chest. I did my best to continue with the meeting and pray for my team. After I finished, I joined my husband and reviewed the letter. Paul was unaffected emotionally by the contents, whereas I felt devastated. Choked up, I read it only once. Copies of the letter had also been sent to a number of our leaders and church members.

BLESSING

I prayed for the senders over the next few days and weeks. Matthew 7:1-2 (AMPC) says: "Do not judge and criticize and condemn others, so that you may not be judged and criticized and condemned yourselves. For just as you judge and criticize and condemn others, you will be judged and criticized and condemned, and in accordance with the measure you [use to] deal out to others, it will be dealt out again to you."

I used Stephen's example in Acts 7:60 and asked God to not hold this against them. Luke 6:28 tells us to bless those who hurt us, so I prayed for the Lord to restore and bless the people who sent the letter. However, forgiveness is not healing, and it does not necessarily deal with fear. After I dealt with the pain that the letter caused, seeing the phrase "Dear Pastors Paul and Jo..." could still leave me shaken. I received a message starting with those words about a month after the letter had been circulated. It took me an hour to pluck up the courage to read the text. It turned out to be a lovely thank you for a birthday card. I was afraid of going through similar pain again.

OVERWHELMED

If you have come under attack, you may have felt overwhelmed by fear. This is especially the case if you have never really conquered concerns about people's opinions. When your reputation is dragged through the mud, it can affect multiple relationships. It can feel like your dirty linen has been washed in public. Maybe your divorce became very public and people said all sorts of things. Perhaps there were problems at work, and you became the fall guy. You may have been the victim of rumors, gossip and accusations and you still dread potential repercussions.

David gave us a model of how we need to handle the fear that arises when we are under attack. He was far from perfect, but he had a pure heart, and he loved the Lord. God always looked after him. In Psalms 31:13-14, he said, "For I hear the slander of many; fear is on every side; while they take counsel together against me, they scheme to take away my life. But as for me, I trust in You, O Lord; I say, 'You are my God.'"

Firstly, David told the Lord about his distress. He shared his anxiety in prayer. However, he did not stop there. Secondly, he told the Lord: "I trust you." He took his eyes off the fray and focused on his Heavenly Father. When we shift our eyes away from the object of our dread and onto the power of God, we immediately reduce the enemy's influence in our lives. Thirdly, David put his faith into words and spoke out loud, "You are my God." By declaring that God was in charge, he was reminding himself and the enemy that he belonged to the Lord of All, and that his life was God's responsibility.

GOD'S PROBLEM

There are many times when I have reminded myself that I am God's problem! That might sound irreverent, yet when my back is against the wall and I don't know what to do, I love to let go of everything and let God take control. One of my husband's favorite phrases is: "God is bigger than the things that are bigger than you!" King David was an expert at running into the arms of the Lord any time he was afraid. Romans 8:31 reads, "What then shall we say to these things? If God is for us, who can be against us?" The greatest relief from fear is remembering who is on our side.

The Lord is not only in your corner, but He made the way for your peace. Isaiah 53:5 (NIV) says: "But he was pierced for our transgressions, he was crushed for our iniquities; the punishment that brought us peace was on him, and by his wounds we are healed." Notice that Jesus was crushed for your sake. He suffered terrible trauma so that you could come into perfect peace.

WALKING IN FREEDOM

I encourage you to identify every way that the enemy has tried to torment, control and hurt you. Maybe you have flashbacks. Perhaps you become anxious in certain settings. Maybe particular people or places raise your stress levels. Are you afraid that the same thing might happen again? Do you avoid sights or sounds that might remind you of the past? Try to identify any ways that fear has tried to torment you or control your behavior. When you know what you are dealing with, it is easier to conquer.

FACE YOUR FEARS

An important step in breaking the power of fear in your life is to face those sights. When flashbacks come, look at the memories that you once ran away from. Experts who treat people with Post Traumatic Stress Disorder agree that revisiting distressing experiences is vital to recovery. As a child of God, you won't be going back to those places alone. You will return to the trauma with the greatest therapist of all time: your Wonderful Counsellor (see Isaiah 9:6).

We are not just called to run into the arms of our Heavenly Father. We are instructed to deal with the fear. Psalms 91:5-6 (NLT) says, "Do not be afraid of the terrors of the night, nor the arrow that flies in the day. Do not dread the disease that stalks in darkness, nor the disaster that strikes at midday." Perhaps if this was being written today, it would say: "Do not be afraid of the thumping footsteps behind you. Do not be afraid of being hated or humiliated. Do not dread cancer, heart attack, or any deadly virus. Do not fear accidents, crashes or disasters." God wants you and me to reach a place where nothing makes us afraid.

My daughter was in a minor car accident that made her afraid of travelling in any vehicle. She had always been slightly scared on road trips, so this crash merely amplified an existing issue. As I wondered why, I began to realize the part I had played. It's not just instinct that says that fear (as well as other emotional issues) can be passed down to the next generation, it's science as well. Epigenetics has shown that non-biological traits can be transmitted. My unresolved problems affected my daughter. Let me explain...

GOING TO THE ROOT

For as long as I could remember, I was a nervous passenger in a car. I inquired of the Lord about the cause. Almost immediately, I remembered something that had taken place thirty-five years earlier. I had fallen asleep in the front seat of a car while a friend was driving me home from an event. We were in the fast lane and travelling at about seventy miles an hour when I awoke in a fright to see us hurtling towards another vehicle. "Jane!" I screamed. It woke up the driver in time for her to slam her foot on the brakes, lessening the impact as we smashed into the other car. Miraculously, neither of us was hurt, but I was terribly distressed. Not knowing how to process trauma, I must have buried the memory. The result: fear found a home in my heart.

As soon as I realized this, I brought the trauma to the Lord in prayer and then dealt with the fear. John 14:27b (AMP) "... Do not let your hearts be troubled, neither let them be afraid. [Stop allowing yourselves to be agitated and disturbed; and do not permit yourselves to be fearful and intimidated and cowardly and unsettled.]" We should not fight fear by running away in dread and calling on the name of the Lord. This scripture is clear. We must not allow ourselves to be agitated. We need to face our fears and refuse to be intimidated.

The next time I was in the car, I glared at huge trucks in neighboring lanes, and quietly but sternly asserted: "I'm not scared!" I no longer tolerated any in-car nerves. I looked them in the face, dismantled any lies I believed, and calmed my heart. I then stopped focusing on anything that would generate anxiety. I refused to stare at other cars. Both driving and being driven became much more enjoyable experiences. My change enabled me to help my daughter to conquer her fears. When we tackle trauma, it improves our lives and it also promotes the well-being of our nearest and dearest.

EXAM JITTERS

Sasha, a lady from London, was due to sit some nursing exams. She was a smart woman who had studied, so she knew everything back to front. However, she kept failing and having to retake exams because fear paralyzed her each time she entered the examination hall. Desperate to graduate, she asked for my help. I asked her to shut her eyes and then I led her in prayer. Once we had honored the presence of God, I asked her to visualize herself entering the huge test center, with her big brother Jesus at her side.

John 8:32 says, "And you shall know the truth, and the truth shall make you free." The Greek for know is ginōskō and it means to be sure, to feel, to understand, and to perceive. This is not head knowledge. It is a deep inner assurance. When you come to know the truth about your situation, freedom will be easy. Let's use spiders as an example. If you are afraid of them, it is the fear of that insect that gives it power in your life. The truth is that (unless you're in the tropics), virtually every spider is completely harmless. You are a towering giant in comparison. The truth is that people who have intimidated you are not all-powerful. They are mere mortals. Places where terrible things have happened are not sinister. You just need to be healed of what happened there. When you *know* the truth deep down, you will be free.

Back to Sasha and her anxieties. An exam room is not a frightening place unless you believe that to be the case. It is just a large hall filled with desks and chairs. In prayer, Sasha saw herself walk straight to her seat, knowing that she was not alone. Once at her desk, she looked around the large room, and then I encouraged her to calmly declare, "I'm not afraid of this place. I'm not scared of the exam. I have the Lord with me, and I have the mind of Christ (see 1 Corinthians 2:16). I've got this and God's got me!"

We then rebuked the spirit of fear. This was very simple now that Sasha had faced (and squashed!) her fears. We spent no more than five or six minutes praying together. At the end of our call, peace reigned once again. Sasha called me a couple of weeks later to share the wonderful news that she had passed her nursing exams with flying colors. Instead of turning away from fears, face them and dismantle any demonic arguments that held you captive. Only turn away when you are no longer intimidated.

REBUKE THE SPIRIT

Fear is a spirit. Although we can feel afraid without being oppressed by the enemy, more often than not, the devil walks through the door opened by shock. The enemy then magnifies the problem. We need to take authority over the spirit of fear. In Luke 10:19, Jesus said, "Behold, I give you the authority to trample on serpents and scorpions, and over all the power of the enemy, and nothing shall by any means hurt you." Jesus has given you authority over all the power of the enemy, and of course that includes fear. It is time to take advantage of the upper hand that God has given you.

James 4:7 provides important insight into how to employ your spiritual authority: "Therefore submit to God. Resist the devil and he will flee from you." There are three parts to this verse. Our authority over the enemy comes from being under the authority of the Most High God. First, we need to submit. That means that we need to surrender afresh to Jesus. When we are afraid, we have taken our eyes off the Lord, and we have given our attention to the enemy's threats. In essence, we have stopped trusting.

The day I realized that fear is a sin was liberating. It helped me to develop a zero-tolerance attitude. Romans 14:23 says, "But he who doubts is condemned... for whatever is not from faith is sin." I encourage you to accept responsibility for allowing fear to find a home in your heart. Say sorry to God for being afraid instead of trusting. This is an important part of submitting to the Lordship of Christ.

Secondly, we need to resist the devil. We need to renounce our relationship with fear and make a determined decision that we will no longer tolerate its influence in our lives. That does not mean that we will no longer have to contend with this enemy. It means that we have declared war and will no longer take it lying down. In Psalms 104:9, we read how God drew clear boundaries for the sea when He created the earth: "You have set a boundary that they may not pass over, that they may not return to cover the earth." That's what we do when we renounce fear. We say, "This far, but no further!"

THE PREREQUISITE

It is important that you fully forgive anyone who had a part to play in your distress. One of the consequences of unforgiveness is that it gives the enemy a legal right to release torment in our lives (see Matthew 18:34). If you have any anger against anyone, lay it down at the cross. Don't forget that holding unforgiveness harms you, not them. My book Doorway to your Destiny has an in-depth teaching on forgiveness that will help you to find freedom.

Once you have forgiven, you can take authority over the spirit of fear and drive it out of your life. I love the last part of our key verse. Let's look at it in The Passion Translation: "So then, surrender to God. Stand up to the devil and resist him and he will turn and run away from you." (James 4:7) When the enemy realizes that you understand and know how to employ your authority over him, he scarpers!

STAYING FREE

There are two tracks to freedom from fear. We need to be relieved of the torment through deliverance, but we must also deal with any remaining fears on a daily basis. Galatians 5:1 (TPT) says, "Let me be clear, the Anointed One has set us free - not partially, but completely and wonderfully free! We must always cherish this truth and stubbornly refuse to go back into the bondage of our past." It is vital that we protect our freedom. Any time you need to face a memory that contains dread, do so. Any time you need to resist the spirit of fear, do it quickly.

The other way to protect your freedom is to develop a healthy response to any type of anxiety. 1 Peter 5:7 (AMPC) guides us through that process: "Casting the whole of your care [all your anxieties, all your worries, all your concerns, once and for all] on Him, for He cares for you affectionately and cares about you watchfully." Any time any type of worry tries to weigh you down, bring it to the Lord in prayer.

Tell Jesus that you are handing over the things that you were worried about to Him because He is well able to manage your problems. If you notice that you are concerned about anything, cast the care upon the Lord. Be quick to tell God what has bothered you, then leave it with Him. If you become anxious about anything, come to God in prayer and hand it all over to the One who cares about every aspect of your life. Let's deal with this foul enemy together. Before we pray, please use the Trauma Tracker on the next page to help identify any fears you need to overcome.

FEAR TRAUMA TRACKER

Use the list below to identify any fears that you face. Put a check mark beside each category that is relevant to you and then identify 1) how frequently and 2) how severely you contend with this issue, on a scale of 1 (hardly ever or very mild) to 5 (often or severe). Ask the Holy Spirit to help you to complete the checklist.

TYPE OF FEAR	FREQUENCY	SEVERITY
☐ Ambulances	_____	_____
☐ Anxiety	_____	_____
☐ Brake lights	_____	_____
☐ Certain words	_____	_____
☐ Dentists	_____	_____
☐ Driving	_____	_____
☐ Flashbacks	_____	_____
☐ Highways	_____	_____
☐ Hospitals	_____	_____
☐ Phone calls	_____	_____
☐ Panic attacks	_____	_____
☐ Places	_____	_____
☐ People	_____	_____
☐ Public speaking	_____	_____
☐ Sirens	_____	_____
☐ Smells	_____	_____
☐ Sounds	_____	_____
☐ Texts	_____	_____
☐ Other................	_____	_____
☐ Other:..............	_____	_____

Take note of the most frequent and severe fears, and deal with these first in prayer. Develop a zero-tolerance attitude towards any fear in your life. And please, keep fighting until you are free. Chapter nine will help you on that journey. Let's pray:

Heavenly Father,

Thank You that You have made the way for me to enjoy complete liberty. Thank You that You are bigger than the things that are bigger than me. You are my God, and You are Lord over all so have Your way in me, I pray.

Facing Distress

Today, I make an important decision. I will no longer turn away from distressing memories or fears. I will no longer bury unpleasant experiences in my soul. I ask for Your help to face every issue that I once feared. (*If there are memories that you have repeatedly avoided, now is the time to open the eyes of your heart and look at the trauma. It may be a horrific accident, seeing a loved one suffer, a public humiliation, a meltdown in an exam - whatever God is reminding you about...*)

Heavenly Father, I went through a terrible experience. It marked me and broke me, but today I look at the memories I once buried. (*Now see yourself back in that place. Share every detail with the Lord in prayer. Remember, He is your Wonderful Counsellor, so He wants you to tell Him everything. He wants to know what happened and how it made you feel.*) From now on, whenever a painful memory comes to mind, I will bring it to You in prayer. I will not allow it to become an object of dread.

Submitting

You are my Lord, and I am Your child. I am sorry for the times that I have been afraid, because fear is sin. I ask for Your forgiveness for tolerating intimidation in my life. I am sorry for the years that I have lived under the influence of fear. Today, I draw a line under that season. I renounce my previous alignment with fear, and from now on, I will face and fight fear until I am completely free. I will not be afraid of people, places, events, memories or anything else.

Forgiving

I choose today to forgive those who have hurt me. What they did was wrong, and it was horrible. They hurt me badly. However, I know that holding anger only holds me back, so I won't do it anymore. You freely forgave me, so I freely forgive those who have wronged me. (*Now mention the people by name that you forgive. Tell God what they did and then let Him know that you don't hold it against them anymore.*) I don't want to be tormented anymore so I close the door on the devil by letting go of every bit of anger and upset. I let you go. You don't owe me anything anymore. I release you. (*If they are alive, continue...*) I ask You to bless those who hurt me (see Matthew 5:44). I ask You to help them, to heal them and to be with them.

Resisting

Now, in the name of Jesus, I take authority over the spirt of fear. Jesus rendered you powerless and I do the same in Jesus' name! I bind you and I drive you out of my life. In the name of Jesus, I command you to leave. I declare that no weapon formed against me will prosper. I am not afraid anymore!

Holy Spirit, please fill me afresh. Flood every area of my heart with Your presence and have Your way in my life. I give You all the praise and all the glory!

In Jesus' name,

Amen.

Chapter 6

PAIN

I ached in places I didn't know existed in the weeks after my daughter died. The agony came in waves. I might have been distracted for a while from the reality of Naomi's untimely departure. Then something would bring me back to earth with a thump, and pain would convulse through my body. I felt like my heart had been plunged to new depths such was the extent of the anguish. At times, I would be overwhelmed by sadness. On other occasions, it was the trauma of her final hours that dominated my thoughts.

Heartache feels terrible, but it also causes lasting damage. Proverbs 4:23 (TPT) says, "So above all, guard the affections of your heart, for they affect all that you are. Pay attention to the welfare of your innermost being, for from there flows the wellspring of life." Your heart makes you who you are, and it influences how you live. When you're crippled by pain, in many ways your life is on pause. If you were having problems with your physical heart, I'm sure you would be quick to seek help. In the same way, it is vital that you take care of your soul.

PHYSICAL EFFECTS

Proverbs 17:22 (AMPC) tells us that: "A happy heart is good medicine, and a cheerful mind works healing, but a broken spirit dries up the bones." When all is well on the inside, there are untold benefits. A happy heart and mind bring healing to your whole body. That's not all, though. Nehemiah 8:10b says that, "... the joy of the Lord is your strength." Inner contentment promotes physical health, and it builds your strength.

The opposite is also true. When a person's spirit is broken, it dries up their bones. The Passion Translation puts Proverbs 17:22 like this: "A joyful, cheerful heart brings healing to both body and soul. But the one whose heart is crushed struggles with sickness and depression." Medical research has caught up with Scripture: a recent study revealed that one in five people who had a major heart attack was suffering from depression. It also showed that among those who were hospitalized afterwards, people suffering from depression were more likely to have another heart attack and pass away. Happiness promotes health, but sadness increases a person's vulnerability to mental illness and sickness. Please take emotional pain seriously.

LOCATING PAIN

Some time back, I went through a painful period in my marriage. I had unwittingly hurt my husband which caused him to shut down. For several months, I felt unwanted. I didn't share the struggles of this season with the people around me because it was very personal. However, I often went for long prayer walks in the countryside where I would share my heart with the Lord. On one of these walks, I noticed that the pain I was feeling was located in my belly. I prayed, cried and got healed. When I got home, I did some research to see if I could find out why my emotional pain was located in my tummy. I was amazed at what I discovered...

You and I do not have just one nervous system. We have two. The second nervous system is located in our gut and is often known as our 'second brain'. It is called the enteric nervous system. This nervous system is connected to our main nervous system via a network of nerves. Because of your enteric nervous system, you can feel stress, pain and other emotions in your gut. Many people have experienced butterflies in their stomach before a big event or diarrhea before public speaking. You feel stress in your gut as a result of the huge network of nerves located there. In fact, there are more nerve cells in your gut than in your entire spinal cord. Also, ninety percent of all the body's serotonin and half the body's dopamine live in your gut. These hormones are responsible in part for your moods and emotions. (My apologies to the doctors reading. I'm sure this is horribly oversimplified!)

The reason I am sharing a little about the enteric nervous system is to make this important point: emotional pain is not just some airy-fairy issue. It is real, and it is physical. Other research shows that nerve receptors react in the same way to emotional as well as physical pain. In other words, nerve receptors will show heightened activity if someone breaks your heart and if you break your arm. Research also proved that medication can relieve the intensity of heartache just as it can relieve body ache. (Of course, medicine can only ever provide temporary relief. The Holy Spirit brings lasting healing.)

REFUSING TO ACCEPT HELP

We are returning to a story that provides important insight into human reactions to pain. We looked at the massacre of toddlers in Bethlehem in Chapter 4 and we will go there again now and also in the next chapter. Matthew 2:16-18 tells the story: "Then Herod... put to death all the male children who were in Bethlehem and in all its districts, from two years old and under...A voice was heard in Ramah, lamentation, weeping, and great mourning, Rachel weeping for her children, refusing to be comforted, because they are no more."

Rachel could not handle the tragedy, so she pushed away any source of comfort. Maybe that is how you feel. You don't want anyone to try to make things right. That may be understandable for a while. However, if it continues for more than a week or two, it is not helpful. Pain is real, so when we push it down it does not go away. Jeremiah 15:18 says: "Why is my pain perpetual and my wound incurable, which refuses to be healed?" Hurts will not be healed without us deliberately seeking restoration. Time does not heal. Jesus does.

You need to be made whole in order to fulfill your God-given potential, but your hidden problems don't just affect you. They have an impact on others as well. If you don't deal with your trauma, it will show up in your most meaningful relationships. Let's look at Proverbs 4:23 (TPT) again. It says, "So above all, guard the affections of your heart, for they affect all that you are. Pay attention to the welfare of your innermost being, for from there flows the wellspring of life." If you struggle to face your pain for your own sake, do it for the sake of those you love.

BURYING THE PAIN

Tamar was King David's daughter. She was a princess with a bright future. All too often, horrible things happen to good individuals. I think that is because the devil detests nice people. Well, something terrible happened to this young lady. Tamar's half-brother Amnon had an all-consuming crush on her and hatched a plan to trick Tamar into his bedroom. This young woman will have trusted her brother. She could not have anticipated what was about to happen. Amnon sent everyone away so that he could be alone with his sister. Then he sexually assaulted her. Tamar pleaded with her brother to stop. No amount of anguish or arguing would deter him. Amnon raped Tamar.

In one horrific attack, Tamar's life changed forever. She was brutally betrayed by the brother she was hoping to help back to health. She was robbed of her innocence. Things then got even worse. Probably disgusted with himself and now with her because she was a reminder of his wrongdoing, Amnon threw his sister out of his house. Tamar felt ashamed, rejected and heartbroken. She ran from Amnon's house in floods of bitter tears. Traumatized and terrified, she turned to another brother, Absalom.

THE POWER OF TEARS

God gave us a powerful release mechanism called crying. When we weep, we offload sorrow. King David, one of the Bible's strongest leaders, cried regularly: "... All night I make my bed swim; I drench my couch with my tears." (Psalms 6:6). Tamar was doing the only thing that she could do at that time. She was weeping. If she had only continued - following in her father David's footsteps and telling the Lord about the pain within - I believe God would have healed her heart.

Absalom did not know how to help his sister. Instead of sitting down with Tamar, listening to her anguish and speaking kindly to her, Absalom said: "But now hold your peace, my sister. He is your brother; do not take this thing to heart." This was horribly wrong for three reasons. First, Absalom told Tamar to hold her peace. Tamar was traumatized. There was no peace to hold.

Second, Absalom suggested his sister should ignore the matter because the perpetrator was her brother. Many people have a deep sense of loyalty that makes them think they must protect family privacy at all costs. If you have been hurt by those who are close, the Lord wants to heal you. It is not dishonoring to admit to God that you were wounded by your relatives. In fact, it is essential that you are honest and ask Him to heal you.

Absalom's third statement was ridiculous. Tamar was broken. This brutal attack had torn her apart. Yet her brother advised her not to take this matter to heart. He was implying that she should stop crying and push down her pain. He told her to internalize her hurt. Perhaps he could not handle the agony of seeing his sister in pain. Maybe he thought that showing anguish was a sign of weakness. It could be that he believed tears would give Amnon another victory. The very next phrase is so sad. "So, Tamar remained desolate." (2 Samuel 13:20b).

SHUT DOWN

Tamar shut down on the inside. She shut her mouth and she shut the world out. She remained desolate for the rest of her life. Sweeping sadness under the carpet does not make it go away. Ignoring distress does not bring relief. It settles in our souls, opening the door to dryness and discouragement. Society often tells us to hide our emotions. Culture teaches us that silence is strength and emotional detachment from pain is a sign of maturity. It can be difficult to talk about our hurts to the Lord, but the rewards are lasting relief.

God has a great plan for your life - to prosper you and give you a bright future. It is important that you know this. However, the devil has a plan too. According to John 10:10, satan wants to kill, steal and destroy. He knows he can't just waltz in and end all our lives. So, he tries to spoil them. Satan seeks to destroy your destiny. He knows that your heart determines the course of your life, so he will do everything in his power to keep you bound with unresolved pain.

NUMBING THE PAIN

We talked about the terrors that Noah must have encountered when the earth was devastated, and his countrymen drowned. It is hardly surprising that one of Noah's first projects after he settled on land was to make wine. Genesis 9:20-21 says, "Noah began to be a farmer, and he planted a vineyard. Then he drank of the wine and was drunk and became uncovered in his tent." Noah was a good man, but he became so intoxicated that he passed out in his own home. I'm not suggesting that alcohol is the answer to trauma. However, escaping from reality can be tempting in the face of terrible distress.

Have you developed habits that you would rather keep a secret? Maybe you turn to alcohol to numb the pain. Perhaps you overeat. You could have some other unhealthy tendency that distracts you from reality. Avoidance has become commonplace with an opioid epidemic sweeping the world. Proverbs 20:1 says, "Wine is a mocker, strong drink is a brawler..." Food, drink, drugs and painkillers provide short term relief. In the long term, they add to the grief.

THE POWER OF AN ENCOUNTER

My husband Paul and I used to minister at a recovery center for addicts. While he was sharing one week, my husband told the story of our daughter's death. He noticed that a man left the room abruptly while he was speaking. Afterwards, one of the workers explained that this man, who was called Craig, had lost his son 24 years earlier. Within three days of his son's death, Craig took heroin for the first time and had been an addict ever since. My husband asked if he could meet this bereaved father.

Shaking, Craig entered the room where Paul was seated. After spending some time talking with him, my husband started to pray. He placed his hand on Craig's chest and asked the Lord to heal the pain that had been buried for decades. Craig started to sob from deep within as sorrow and grief poured out of his heart. Afterwards, he was stunned. Craig explained that he felt years of pain drain away while my husband prayed and then he felt peace fill his heart. For twenty-four years, Craig had veiled the agony with drugs. Then in one supernatural healing encounter, the Lord God took a great deal of that pain away.

If you have been numbing pain or plugging a void, I encourage you to ask the Lord to bypass the substitutes and begin a fresh work in the depths of your heart. Too many addictions are triggered by trauma. Until the deep-rooted pain is released, breaking the habit is very difficult. Healing paves the way for freedom. Hebrews 12:13 says, "Make straight paths for your feet, so that what is lame may not be dislocated, but rather be healed." Instead of beating yourself up every time you fall, surrender every part of your heart to the Lord and ask Him to restore you from the inside out.

WHEN PAIN TURNS TO RAGE

Unresolved agony often manifests itself as anger. This is common when someone has done you a terrible wrong and you don't know what to do with the mix of emotions. At the age of twelve, Terry's world was torn apart. He woke up one night at boarding school to find an older student on top of him. Terrified, Terry was about to cry out when the man muffled his mouth and threatened him: "If you breathe a word to anyone, I will kill you." He froze until the ordeal ended and the man left.

Terry lay awake traumatized for most of the night, unable to fathom what had just happened. After some disturbed sleep, he showered, desperate to clean off the shame and terror. But they could not be washed away. A couple of weeks later, Terry was raped by another man. In total, he was raped five times before he was fourteen. Proverbs 10:23 says, "To do evil is like sport to a fool..." Like Terry, maybe you've experienced cruel games being played by the people around you. If you felt like the prey while others appeared to be predators, God wants to heal every hurt in your heart. I don't know what you have gone through, but I do know that your Heavenly Father is able to restore you.

Perhaps you were abused by people who should have protected you. Maybe you were raped (even repeatedly). You could have been molested or assaulted. You may have been the victim of violence or torture. Whatever you have gone through, I want you to know that you can come out the other side restored.

Terry had frequent flashbacks and couldn't sleep at night for fear of being attacked again. He was expelled from school for doing badly in his exams and soon became extremely angry. Rage boiled inside. He started to fight with his dad. He was completely out of control and felt no connection with anyone. He went on to marry, but anger still controlled his life and now his relationship as he became an abusive husband.

TEMPERED BUT NOT RESOLVED

After he gave his life to the Lord, Terry was still filled with pain and rage. When he was in his early thirties, Terry attended his first healing conference. Sitting in a small group, my husband Paul had a word of knowledge that someone was carrying the burden of a painful childhood memory. For the first time in the twenty years since the brutal assaults, Terry shared his story. He broke down and wept. That marked the start of his healing journey.

Ecclesiastes 3:1-4 tells us that God has set apart a time for healing: "To everything there is a season, a time for every purpose under heaven... a time to break down... a time to weep..." We prepare for our restoration by facing the truth that we have tried so hard to avoid. When the pain flooded out, the anger lost its grip. Having been bound by rage, Terry began his walk to freedom. More often than not, healing begins when we open up. Suppressed pain comes pouring out. If you feel buried sadness surfacing, please don't push it back down. Pain is always better out than in.

DON'T SUFFER IN SILENCE

King David cried out to God about rejection, betrayal, backstabbing, grief and much more. This mighty warrior often shared his emotional pain with God. However, I am not aware of him ever praying about physical hurts - even though he must have experienced these as a soldier. Talking about a gash or a fracture will not bring relief. By contrast, describing inner pain is necessary for restoration. The 'man after God's own heart' did not bottle up his pain. Throughout his life, David acknowledged when he was hurt and brought his sadness to the Lord in prayer.

In Psalm 55, David shared the shock he felt when his dear friend betrayed him at the moment when he needed support the most. Psalm 55:4-5 is part of his prayer: "My heart is severely pained within me, and the terrors of death have fallen upon me. Fearfulness and trembling have come upon me, and horror has overwhelmed me." As we have already seen, trauma is a terrible mix of pain and shock. I think this passage shows how David dealt with trauma. He refused to bury the hurt or turn away from the horror. He put his pain into words and shared every fear with the Lord. Before we pray, please use the Trauma Tracker on the next page to help identify any unhealthy reactions to pain that you need to address to help you to be healed.

PAIN TRAUMA TRACKER

Use the list below to identify any unhealthy ways you have dealt with pain. Put a check mark beside each category that is relevant to you and then identify (if you can) which painful or traumatic experience made you react this way. Ask the Holy Spirit to help you complete the checklist.

REACTION TO PAIN	TRAUMA
☐ Anger (pain has turned to anger)	_____
☐ Alcohol abuse	_____
☐ Avoid talking about painful issues	_____
☐ Bite lip to stop tears	_____
☐ Bury pain	_____
☐ Detach from pain	_____
☐ Drugs abuse	_____
☐ Numb pain with alcohol or substance	_____
☐ Overeat to ease pain	_____
☐ Push pain down	_____
☐ Prescription drugs to numb pain	_____
☐ Rage (pain has turned to rage)	_____
☐ Refuse to be comforted	_____

☐ Self harm e.g. cutting _____

☐ Shut down inside _____

☐ Swallow to subdue sadness _____

☐ Other _____

I would love to lead you in prayer.

Heavenly Father,

I want the rest of my life to be fruitful. I long to be a channel of blessing to those I love, so I ask You to uncover buried pain in my heart. I choose to pursue my healing for the sake of my purpose, but also for the sake of those that I love. I am sorry for the times that I have held onto my pain as a right. I surrender today.

Forgive me for the times that I have dismissed emotional pain as unimportant. I realize now that my heart is very precious, and my inner well-being is vital. Where I have buried hurt, detached myself or shut down in the past, I choose instead to open up my heart to You. Help me to release pain in a healthy way from now on. I give You access to every corner of my heart.

I surrender anything that I have used to numb the pain. (*If you have used food, drink, drugs, tobacco or any other substance to numb pain, right now give your habit to the Lord as an offering.*) I do not want to disguise hurts or cover over wounds. Instead, I ask You to start a deep work of healing in me.

If my pain turned into anger, I ask You to go to the root of my negative passion. Unearth the agony and help me to release my pain in Your presence.

I want to learn to deal with pain the right way, Lord. (*Referring to the Pain Trauma Tracker, ask God to help you overcome every unhealthy reaction you have had to pain*). I will no longer ignore my hurts. I will seek Your help until I am made whole. I will not suffer in silence. I will come to you and pour out my heart before Your face.

I surrender to Your love. I ask You to have Your wonderful way in my life.

In Jesus' name, I pray,

Amen.

Chapter 7

BARRIERS

The enemy wants to keep you trapped by the past. He throws obstacles in your way to stop you moving forward into your healing. These blockages are disguised as 'reasons' why you can't or shouldn't receive your healing. We are told of the importance of refusing any thought or idea that opposes God's word in 2 Corinthians 10:5: "Casting down arguments and every high thing that exalts itself against the knowledge of God, bringing every thought into captivity to the obedience of Christ." In this verse, one of satan's most powerful weapons is exposed. The devil tries to build arguments in our hearts that will cause us to resist (usually unwittingly) the help of God. If the enemy can make me resist heaven's solutions, then his work is done.

After trauma, satan seeks to sow ideas in our minds that are designed to keep us bound up by pain. Before we go any further, I encourage you to stop for a moment and ask the Holy Spirit to reveal any false arguments that you have been believing. We will now deal with some of the most common barriers, one at a time.

1. WHERE WERE YOU?

Lazarus, Martha and Mary were siblings from a town called Bethany. They were very good friends with Jesus. When you are close to someone, it can create expectations. We all have assumptions about how our friends and family will behave in different situations. For example, you may love everyone, but not just anyone can come to your home. That's a privilege reserved for your nearest and dearest. At times of need, we expect close friends to offer their support. Martha and Mary were desperate one day, so they asked their friend Jesus to help.

Let's pick up the story in John 11:1-4, 6 (NLT), "A man named Lazarus was sick. He lived in Bethany with his sisters, Mary and Martha. This is the Mary who poured the expensive perfume on the Lord's feet and wiped them with her hair. Her brother, Lazarus, was sick. So, the two sisters sent a message to Jesus telling him, 'Lord, your dear friend is very sick.' Although Jesus loved Martha, Mary, and Lazarus, He stayed where He was for the next two days."

The Bible reminds us that this is the Mary who gave everything she had to Jesus. The perfume that she poured over His feet was extremely expensive. Historians suggest it was equal to a year's wages. When we give a great deal, even if our giving is entirely motivated by love, it can make us feel that those on the receiving end owe us a debt. Let's apply that argument to our relationship with God. If we have laid our entire lives down for the Lord, then it can create a sense of entitlement. If we don't get the result that we wanted, we can feel cheated.

THE BIG LETDOWN

Notice how Mary communicated with Jesus. She said, "Your dear friend is very sick." However, instead of leaving immediately, Jesus stayed where He was for another two days. While He delayed, Martha and Mary's beloved brother Lazarus died. When Jesus eventually reached Bethany, he had been dead for four days. Mary and Martha were heartbroken. Not only that, they were bewildered that Jesus did not come when they asked. It is highly likely that the sisters had talked about their disappointment because Martha and Mary expressed their confusion at His delay, using the exact same words.

In John 11:21, we read: "Now Martha said to Jesus, 'Lord, if You had been here, my brother would not have died.'" A few verses later in John 11:32-33, we hear the exact same phrase, "When Mary came where Jesus was, and saw Him, she fell down at His feet, saying to Him, 'Lord, if You had been here, my brother would not have died.'" These precious women could not understand why Jesus did not come. They felt abandoned by the only One who could have helped. Their brother's Friend did not come when he needed Him the most.

I don't know how many times I wondered where God was after my daughter died. At the time that Naomi passed away, my husband and I were serving the Lord with all of our hearts, pastoring a small but growing church in London, England. I could not understand why the Lord allowed her to die. He is all-powerful and could have intervened. We had prayed for other sick children in desperate circumstances and watched God heal them. So why did our daughter have to die? Does this sound familiar? Do you feel like God let you down, or maybe it was the church? Perhaps you gave your best like Mary and felt abandoned at your time of greatest need. That can add so much pain to the agony that you are already facing. If that's you, please take a moment to acknowledge your sense of disappointment right now.

2. IF ONLY...

King David was repeatedly betrayed by different people. It was after one of his closest friends and most trusted advisors abandoned him that he poured out his pain in prayer. It wasn't just sadness that he expressed. He wished he could make it all disappear. King David wanted to run away and hide from reality. In Psalms 55:6-7 David cried out, "Oh, that I had wings like a dove! I would fly away and be at rest. Indeed, I would wander far off, and remain in the wilderness." He wanted to escape the pain. He wanted to run from reality and pretend that it had not happened. Unfortunately, a refusal to face reality keeps us trapped.

Professionals who help people with post-traumatic stress disorder agree that the way to lasting relief is to look back at every distressing memory as often as possible. They try to help their clients become desensitized to the trauma so that it loses its power over their lives. It is the same for you and me. In order to be healed, we need to be willing to accept reality and face our pain. When we spend our time wishing that the trauma had never happened, or wishing that we could escape, we are merely delaying our healing. Maybe you find yourself wishing that that fateful day had never happened. Perhaps you know that deep inside you have struggled to accept that it is really over. Although it is difficult to face the painful truth, it is the only way ahead.

Another Bible hero that wished he could change his circumstances was Job. I don't think anyone has suffered loss or trauma like Job. He lost all his children in a freak accident one night. In the weeks after his terrible tragedy, he wished he could turn back the clock and return to the days before everything went wrong. In Job 29:2,5-6, this grief-stricken father lamented, "Oh, that I were as in months past, as in the days when God watched over me... When the Almighty was yet with me, when my children were around me; when my steps were bathed with cream, and the rock poured out rivers of oil for me!" He longed to be able to return to the good old days. He would have done anything to travel back in time.

Maybe you long to go back for just one day. You pine for the opportunity to revisit the weeks before everything went horribly wrong. Do you keep returning in your heart to the times when all was well and try to remain in that place for as long as possible before reality bites? Of course, we need to remember the good times. However, if we long to go back then we are living in a fantasy land that will only make things harder in the long run. Truth is always the way to healing and freedom.

3. BRANDED BY TRAGEDY

A woman in the Old Testament called Naomi suffered terribly. She went with her husband and their two sons to the land of Moab to escape a famine back home in Judah. While living in a foreign country, Naomi's husband and then both her sons Mahlon and Kilion died. She lost everything that was precious to her. Ruth 1:4b-5 (NLT) says, "But about ten years later, both Mahlon and Kilion died. This left Naomi alone, without her two sons or her husband." Eventually, Naomi decided to head back home to Bethlehem, bringing her daughter-in-law Ruth with her.

We will pick up the story in Ruth 1:19b-21 (NLT): 'When they came to Bethlehem, the entire town was excited by their arrival. "Is it really Naomi?" the women asked. "Don't call me Naomi," she responded. "Instead, call me Mara, for the Almighty has made life very bitter for me. I went away full, but the Lord has brought me home empty. Why call me Naomi when the Lord has caused me to suffer and the Almighty has sent such tragedy upon me?'

Notice that Naomi had been branded by her tragedy. Her name in the Hebrew means pleasant, or my delight. She did not want people to use that name any longer. Instead, she asked them to call her Mara, which means bitter. Trauma had changed her view of herself and marked her identity. She viewed herself as a widow and a bereaved mother. That was what shaped her inner image. Proverbs 23:7 says, "For as he thinks in his heart, so is he." In other words, your inner opinion frames your life. Your heart thoughts become self-fulfilling prophecies. If deep down I see myself as a victim of trauma, then it will be difficult to be restored. My own inner image will be working against me.

VICTIM MOTHER

In the years after my daughter died, I went on to have a son and another daughter. Yet I still saw myself as a victim mother. Not only had my first child died, but Abby, who was now my youngest, had suffered a great deal as a result of complex health issues. This made me think that I was different. I saw myself as someone that had been to hell and back and come out the other side. I felt entitled to special treatment. I thought that I should be allowed (even if only occasionally) to engage in self-pity without consequences.

I will never forget the day that the Lord lovingly changed my perspective. God showed me a picture of myself. I was carrying my daughters - one on each hip - and my son was standing at my feet. He asked me to embrace and then entrust each child to Him. First, I cuddled my beautiful baby girl, Naomi, and then I gave her over to the Lord. Next, I wrapped my arms around my precious Abby, kissed her and placed her in the arms of the Lord. Finally, I picked up my little champion, Benjy. I hugged him and then handed him to my Heavenly Father. Immediately afterwards, I heard the Lord say, "You are not a victim mother. You are my treasured daughter." Something broke off me. My perspective changed and I was set free from a victim mentality. I realized that my identity was forged by the love of my Father, and not by tragedy.

If you realize that trauma has marked the way you see yourself, the Lord wants to wash the sadness away. No event should have the power to forge your identity. Perhaps you see yourself as a victim of abuse, cruelty or negligence. Maybe you picture yourself as an orphan, a widow, or even a divorcee. It could be that some other circumstance has marked you. When our inner picture is of a victim, it will affect all our relationships and influence the way we live. When we break out of a victim mindset, we set ourselves up for a better life. The Lord wants you to know that you are marked by His love, not by trauma. Song of Songs 2:4 says: "He brought me to the banqueting house, and His banner over me was love." When your inner picture of yourself changes, your life will start to improve.

4. IT'S HIS FAULT

Naomi, whose story is told in the book of Ruth, was like many of us. She wasn't contending with just one inner argument. She was stuck as a result of two. Let's go back to Ruth 1:21 (NLT) and look again at what she said to her friends in Bethlehem: "I went away full, but the Lord has brought me home empty. Why call me Naomi when the Lord has caused me to suffer and the Almighty has sent such tragedy upon me?" Naomi thought that God was her problem. She believed that the Lord caused her pain. Seeing the All-Powerful One as the source of your sadness will inevitably lead to a terrible sense of hopelessness. If you believe that the Lord of All is against you, then there is no way out. It is a crippling lie that the devil uses to hurt God's people.

Job believed that lie and it nearly poisoned him: "For the arrows of the Almighty are within me; my spirit drinks in their poison..." (Job 6:4). The Lord God is the only One who can provide lasting help, so if we see Him as the problem, we will probably be stuck in a desolate place. If you believe that He was responsible for your suffering, I would love to help lead you out of that darkness and pain. There will be a prayer at the end of this chapter that will help you on your way. I know that we don't have all the answers this side of heaven. I can't explain why you had to suffer so much. But I know for sure that God is a good Father who only wants the best for you. James 1:17 (MSG) says, "Every desirable and beneficial gift comes out of heaven. The gifts are rivers of light cascading down from the Father of Light. There is nothing deceitful in God, nothing two-faced, nothing fickle." He is for you.

5. WHY?

About four months after our daughter died, I told a dear friend, "When I can understand why Naomi had to die, then I can start to heal." It was so unfair that our child had gone. We had done everything to protect her throughout her short life. We prayed over her health and watched our words. We were full of faith for her future to be bright. So why did our little girl have to die? What did we do wrong? Why her, why us, why me? I was tormented and I was stuck.

It was at that time that I heard the Lord ask me an important question. "Could there ever be a good enough reason why your daughter had to die?" I paused for some time before responding. "No. There is no reason that could ever be good enough for why our little girl died." It was at that moment that I understood the mess that I was in. My questions were only adding to the chaos of my mind and they held my heart ransom. With tears streaming down my cheeks, I made the monumental decision to give up my questions, to let go of my 'why' and to lay down my right to an answer. That marked the beginning of my healing journey.

We cannot understand everything. There are a multitude of mysteries that are beyond our control and comprehension. Searching for reasons for your suffering is (more often than not) counterproductive and just creates greater confusion. It rarely leads to restoration or freedom. If you are in turmoil, I encourage you to lay it all down. Please hand over every sense of injustice. Give God all your questions and surrender the confusion. When you let go, you will be able to receive His healing love. The Lord is able to help when your heart is open and available.

6. IT'S A WRITE-OFF

Most of us live our lives according to unwritten rules and believe unspoken ideologies. One of them is this: there are some things so bad that we will never fully recover from them. Although you may not have thought about it before, you might subconsciously see certain outcomes as impossible. For example, if you heard about a woman who was sexually abused all her life, you may believe that she could be saved and find peace. However, you may doubt that she could ever have a healthy and fulfilling sex life.

Remember Rachel whose story we have already studied in Matthew 2:18b? "Rachel weeping for her children, refusing to be comforted, because they are no more." Something inside this grief-stricken woman was refusing the comfort that she so desperately needed. She was pushing away help because there was nothing that anyone could do to bring her sons back from the dead. She did not want anyone to try to make her feel better because she was bereaved.

Now apply that principle to your own life. Have you assumed that any terrible trauma will be with you forever? Have you believed that you will always have a problem in some area of your life as a result of a calamity? Have you thought that you will always have to carry some sort of sorrow or sadness? After we lost our daughter, many people (both in church ministry and secular life) told us that we would never fully recover after the loss of a child. The assumption was that we would learn to live with the pain and that we would always miss our daughter. After all, she was our flesh and blood.

That sounds reasonable. However, after searching the scriptures, I did not find any verse that says that certain traumas are too much for the Lord to heal. I cannot find a story that demonstrates that some 'emotional giants' are too big for God. Jesus came from heaven to earth with a mission, and part of that mission was to minister healing to your heart. Isaiah 61:1b (AMPC) says: "... He has sent me to bind up and heal the brokenhearted..." Again, we read in Psalms 147:3 (AMPC) that: "He heals the brokenhearted and binds up their wounds [curing their pains and their sorrows]." The Bible says that God *cures* our hurts. When something is cured, it no longer causes *any* problems.

NOTHING IS OFF LIMITS!

There is nothing that you have gone through - no abuse, no violence, no trauma, no tragedy - that God cannot completely heal. He is able to take *all* your pain away and remove *every* trace of sadness. Isaiah 53:5b (NLT) is clear: "He was beaten so we could be whole." When we are whole, nothing is missing. The AMPC version of Isaiah 53:5b says: "...with the stripes [that wounded] Him we are healed and made whole." Healing is relief in one area or another, whereas wholeness is when the work is finished! The dictionary definition of whole is: 'complete; all elements properly belonging; not broken, damaged, or impaired in any way.' You can be made whole!

There is only one requirement. For you to be completely healed, you need to surrender all your hurts to Him. You may wonder what I mean? How do we *give up* our pain? That's the kind of language which is usually used when speaking about your rights. I will explain in a moment, but first, I want you to know that your heart is deep. Psalms 64:6b says, "...Both the inward thought and the heart of man are deep." You have thoughts so deep that you may not even be aware of them. The word 'inward' used in this verse also means 'heart' in the Hebrew. Your heart thoughts affect your decisions and the way you live (see Proverbs 23:7), but sometimes you're not even aware that they are there...

Let me explain what I mean by *giving up* pain. When we feel wronged by the terrible things that we have experienced, sometimes we want to hold on to our hurts. The sense of injustice makes us feel entitled to hanging on to part of our pain. Maybe you worry deep down that if you were to be completely healed, then it might somehow suggest that your suffering was acceptable. Perhaps you think that your wounds somehow hold someone to account for what happened. In truth, all these unsaid inner arguments are just blockages to your restoration. When you surrender every source of sadness, it is a sign of total trust. The response of your loving Lord will be immediate. He will start to put your broken heart back together, one precious piece at a time.

THE WAY AHEAD

Are you ready to receive a different miracle? I promise you that it is still powerful, and it is very precious, but it might not be the miracle that you originally wanted. As you know, our first daughter died, but our other daughter was brought back from the brink of death three times. I will be forever grateful to God for saving Abby's life. She is not only my remarkable daughter. She is my dear friend. When I share the stories of the restoration of me and my husband after Naomi's death as well as Abby's physical healings, it is the healing of our hearts that impacts people the most. The healing I didn't originally ask for (and really didn't want) is the one that has helped multitudes. If you will allow the Lord to restore every part of your heart, you will be made whole. You may also discover that you have a story to tell that will give hope to the hopeless.

I would love to help you to dismantle every obstacle to your future well-being. Psalms 39:4-5 (NLT) says: "Lord, remind me how brief my time on earth will be. Remind me that my days are numbered—how fleeting my life is. You have made my life no longer than the width of my hand. My entire lifetime is just a moment to you; at best, each of us is but a breath." Life is short, and in the twinkling of an eye, we will be enjoying glory. You have an opportunity to make the time you have here count. As you destroy every argument that has held you back, you will pave the way for your restoration, and you will position yourself to fulfill your God-given destiny. I would love to lead you in prayer. First, though, please use the Trauma Tracker on the next page to help identify any obstacles that have been preventing your total healing.

BLOCKAGES TRAUMA TRACKER

Use the list below to identify any obstacles that might be getting in the way of your progress. Put a check mark beside each category that is relevant to you and then identify which traumatic experience(s) has made you feel this way. Ask the Holy Spirit to help you to complete the checklist.

ARGUMENTS OR OBSTACLES

CAUSED BY TRAUMA(S)

☐ Avoid the pain _____

☐ Branded by trauma _____

☐ Hold onto my pain _____

☐ God is against me _____

☐ I don't understand why _____

☐ I will always feel pain _____

☐ It's not fair _____

☐ Let down by God _____

☐ Let down by people _____

☐ Struggle to accept reality _____

☐ Too broken to fix _____

☐ Victim identity _____

☐ Wish it never happened _____

☐ Other _____

☐ Other _____

These issues may not all apply to you, but join me in praying through each one anyway.

Heavenly Father,

I don't want the past to hold me back any longer, so I ask for Your help to remove any obstacles that have been preventing my progress. Please help me to recognize and cast down any inner argument that has held me captive.

Let Down - Like Martha and Mary, I have felt let down. I felt abandoned by (*now tell the Lord who you felt abandoned you. If you felt let down by Him, let Him know*). It hurt and confused me, Lord. It was so wrong, and it felt unjust. I have carried this rock in my heart for too long, but today I choose to lay it down. I let go of the letdown. I give up every sense of injustice. I release it once and for all into Your hands, Oh Lord.

If Only - I have often wished everything could be different. I have longed to go back to the way it once was. I wished I could turn back the clock. But now I realize that longing for what I can't have will only keep me bound. So today, I accept my reality. I stop wishing I could go back, and instead, I ask You to walk with me through the pain and heal me. Thank You that You have a good plan for my life. Heal my heart, I pray.

Identity - Trauma has affected my view of myself. I have seen myself as a victim. I have identified myself with tragedy and difficulty. I realize that Your will is that I see myself only as Your child, marked by Your love. (*Now give the Lord any people or wounds that have forged a victim identity. Tell Him how you have seen yourself and then hand over your old identity to the Lord.*) Thank You, Lord, that I am your dearly loved child. That is who I am.

Blaming God - Heavenly Father, I am so sorry that I have held you responsible in some way for my pain. I thought You were part of my problem, but I was wrong. You are a good, good Father, and You only want the best for me. I now know that my pain was not

Your will. I don't understand why it all happened, but I know that You are not to blame. You are my only hope, so I ask for Your forgiveness. I ask that You heal my heart.

Why? - I don't understand why I had to suffer so much. It feels so wrong that I have had to endure so much. It is not right that the people I love have also had to go through so much pain (*Now tell the Lord exactly what was so unjust.*) I don't understand what went wrong but I realize that no answer could ever be good enough. So, I choose today to give up my right to know. I let go of all my questions and confusions. I give up my right to an answer. I give up 'Why?' I no longer want answers. I only want Your healing love.

Off limits - Father, I thank You that there is no pain or tragedy that You cannot heal. You are more than able to heal me and to make me whole. So today, I surrender every sadness, every sorrow, every hurt in my heart to You. I open up every part of my heart to You and I ask You to heal me everywhere I hurt. Have Your way in me. I choose to seek my restoration with all of my heart. I will no longer hold onto any reasons why I cannot be healed. I choose to lay them down. Instead, I ask You to start a new work in me.

In Jesus' name, I pray,

Amen.

CURES

Trauma is devastating, but through His death and resurrection, Jesus made the way for you to have an abundant life. He suffered unimaginable pain so that you could be healed. He destroyed the devil's power so that you could be more than a conqueror. In this section, you will experience the healing and freedom that Jesus died to provide.

Chapter 8

HEALING

Rage and violence dominated Raquel's home. Every day, her mom gave her verbal attacks and beatings. By age five, Raquel had learned to detach herself from her emotions. She hardly ever spoke. After becoming a Christian at nineteen, Raquel continued to carry pain deep within. Small remarks would really upset her. She would feel attacked during disagreements and at a loss for words in challenging discussions. Raquel felt like everything was tightly shut within. She didn't even have the vocabulary to express herself emotionally. Raquel explained, "I couldn't remember many of the traumas I went through. It was as though those memories were locked away, out of reach, and yet they wore me down daily."

Raquel attended our two day Healed for Life conference. During one of the sessions, the Holy Spirit took her back to when she was five. "I saw myself as a little girl. All I could hear were the awful words of worthlessness spoken over me. I thought I was ugly. I could hear myself telling that little girl, 'I hate you!' Then the healing began." From the depths of her heart, she cried and poured out pain that had been buried for decades. As the dam burst, she felt God's love like never before. Since that time, although she has remained on her healing journey, Raquel has felt an inner peace that she didn't even realize was available.

IT WON'T GO BUT IT MIGHT GROW

Pain does not disappear if it is ignored. It may be buried, but it will eventually surface. This usually happens under the spotlight of your closest relationships. Left untreated, pain won't go. However, it might grow. Psalms 25:17 says, "The troubles of my heart have enlarged; bring me out of my distresses!" If you leave a bodily wound untreated, it can get infected and become a bigger problem. Emotional hurts are the same. Sometimes ignoring your pain makes it worse.

Let me explain by using an example. If you were criticized by your boss in front of your co-workers, you would probably feel humiliated. If you buried those emotions because they were too unpleasant to face, and instead just trivialized the trauma, you might think you were fine. However, if you then went to a party where a friend asked you a personal question publicly, you could experience undue anxiety. You might then be asked to give a presentation. Something like that which normally wouldn't have bothered you suddenly makes you incredibly stressed. Without realizing it, everything can be traced back to that one unpleasant experience in the office. Please decide today that you will deal with any pain that the Holy Spirit brings to the surface for the sake of your future well-being.

Job 5:7 says, "Yet man is born to trouble, as the sparks fly upward." When metal is being molded, sparks *always* fly upwards. In the same way, you and I *will* go through distressing times. Jesus called them the storms of life. The Hebrew for trouble here is âmâl and it means misery, sorrow and pain. If trauma is inevitable, we need to know how to be healed *every* time it happens.

UNIQUELY YOURS

Your heart is unique. Just as no two people have identical fingerprints, so no one else has a heart like yours. Psalms 33:15 says, "He fashions their hearts individually..." There are probably times when you feel like no one understands your pain or what you have been through. That's true: they could not fathom how you're feeling because they aren't you. The only One who knows exactly what is going on inside is the Lord. He understands all your inner churning and He knows your pain. He knows every hidden secret of your heart (see Psalms 44:21b). Even when you aren't sure why you feel a certain way, He knows. Speaking of Jesus, John 2:25 (NLT) says, "... He knew what was in each person's heart."

I don't know which traumatic experiences still cause you to recoil, but God knows. Maybe it was the breakdown of your marriage. Perhaps it was a terrible accident. Or it could be a horrific hospital appointment. Lamentations 3:20 says, "My soul still remembers and sinks within me." What causes your heart to sink? The Lord wants to do a deep work on the inside and restore your heart. Any memory that still stings is a memory that your Heavenly Father wants to restore. He does not want to leave any wound untreated. Jesus wants to heal you anywhere you hurt.

IF IT HURTS YOU, IT HURTS HIM TOO

One of the lies that the devil wants you to believe is that God is not bothered by your pain. If the enemy can't successfully convince you that the Lord was the author of your agony, he will try to make you believe that God is detached from your feelings. If you picture Him as your boss, or even worse, as your judge, you may think that He does not care about your heart. This is about as far from the truth as you could get.

Jeremiah 8:21says, "For the hurt of the daughter of my people I am hurt..." Let those words sink deep down. Your Heavenly Father hurts when *you* hurt. Just as the average earthly parent is distressed when their child is in pain, so your Heavenly Father is grieved by your trauma. You are His child. He cares about every aspect of your life. He longs for you to be restored.

When my children were small, there were times when my husband would kneel with his arms open wide and call to Benj or Abby, "Come for a cuddle!" He would then scoop them up in the most loving hug. Your Heavenly Father adores you with greater affection than any earthly father ever could. Jeremiah 31:3b says, "I have loved you with an everlasting love; therefore, with lovingkindness I have drawn you". The Lord loves you. As a result, He hurts when you hurt and longs for you to be made whole.

UNLOCKING THE DOOR TO YOUR HEART

Your heart is deep and complex, like a huge house with many secret rooms. When something hurtful happens, it is as though a room inside your soul gets blocked with pain. We need to invite the Holy Spirit to shine His light into our hearts to uncover buried wounds. Proverbs 20:27 (TPT) says, "The spirit God breathed into man is like a living lamp, a shining light searching into the innermost chamber of our being." The way to unlock the door to inner chambers bound with pain is to invite the presence of God into every corner of your heart and into every memory. Please don't turn away from the pain. Face it, knowing that the Holy Spirit is by your side.

We were designed with a connection between our hearts and our mouths. God speaks what is in His heart, and we were made the same way. Matthew 12:34b says, "... For out of the abundance of the heart the mouth speaks." That is the way you and I were created. The issues of your heart need to be released through your mouth. If you do not vocalize distress, words get trapped and pain gets buried. As a result, hurts are usually bound up by unspoken words.

Once you have returned to a memory with the help of the Holy Spirit, give voice to your pain. Tell the Lord what you went through and how it made you feel. Share it in as much detail as you can. As you face those uncomfortable experiences, and tell the Lord how they affected you, pain will be unearthed, and tears will usually flow. When your pour out your heart to a friend, you share personal information about your life. Psalms 62:8b says, "... Pour out your heart before Him." A friend may listen, but the Lord is able to take every trace of pain away.

YOUR EVER-PRESENT COUNSELOR

Counseling works when a client shares their memories (and the feelings associated with them) with their counselor. In Isaiah 9:6 we are told that Jesus is our *Wonderful Counselor*. What a privilege! Jesus is your ever-present, perfectly attentive Counselor. He always understands and is overflowing with insight. If natural counseling helps, just imagine how effective it will be for you to seek supernatural counseling. The Lord wants you to talk to Him about every difficult detail. As you share how you felt, He will lift your burdens and relieve your distress. When you pour out your heart like water before Him, He will fill you back up with His healing love.

Although others may have ignored your concerns, He wants to hear your voice. He will give you all the time you need. He won't rush you and He won't switch off while you are sharing your heart. The Song of Songs is considered by many to be a story depicting God's love for His people. Listen to the heart of the Lord for you: "O my dove, in the clefts of the rock, in the secret places of the cliff, let me see your face, let me hear your voice; for your voice is sweet, and your face is lovely." (Song of Songs 2:14). Maybe you think that no one is interested in your problems and that no one has the time to listen. Your Heavenly Father wants to hear your heart. He wants to have a long overdue one-to-one with you. He will listen while you share.

Perhaps you have felt dismissed by the people you went to for help. Maybe they shut you down because they didn't know how to handle your pain. You may even need to be healed for the way you were treated in your darkest season. Either way, the Lord wants you to know that He will never minimize the things that weigh you down. He will not make you feel small. His desire is to see you come through strong. Matthew 12:20 (TPT) says, "He won't brush aside the bruised and broken. He will be gentle with the weak and feeble, until his victory releases justice."

THE EXIT DOOR

Your heart was not designed to house pain. Your soul was made for the giving and receiving of love. It was made for fellowship. Allowing hurts to remain in your heart would be like giving strangers permission to live in your house. Pain doesn't belong in your soul any more than squatters belong in your home. As a result, the Lord created an eviction mechanism for pain called crying. When our tears are directed correctly, they bring relief.

Just crying will not normally change anything. Many people weep out of frustration or hurt without getting healed. However, when we learn how to pour out our hearts before the face of the Lord, we will be made whole. I have had the privilege of leading countless people across the world to restoration. People of all ages and backgrounds who have suffered terrible trauma have been healed when they have released their pain in the presence of God.

I often see folk working hard to hold back. I can't tell you how many times people have apologized to me for crying while I'm ministering to them. However, the ability to weep is a gift from God to enable you to release your pain. Ecclesiastes 3:1 says, "To everything there is a season, a time for every purpose under heaven." A list of life's essential purposes follow, then in verses 3 and 4 it says, "... A time to break down... A time to weep..." If you're reading this book, and past trauma is surfacing, then this is that time. Please don't bite your lip, swallow hard or do anything else to try to subdue the pain. Let it out before the Lord.

LETTING GO

There is a big difference between a few tears and pouring out pain. In Psalm 18:6, David said, "I cried out to You in my distress... and... you heard my troubled cry. My sobs came right into Your heart and You turned Your face to rescue me." (TPT). Crying *out* is not the same as crying. When we cry out, there is a thrust behind our tears and agony leaves. Crying is simply tears falling. After trauma, there is usually a reservoir of pain trapped inside. It needs to be released. David knew how to let go in God's presence. In Psalms 6:6 (NLT), he said, "I am worn out from sobbing. All night I flood my bed with weeping, drenching it with my tears." When you have suffered a great deal, you need to pour out your pain in prayer.

Another important point is that crying bitter tears is not the same as surrendering your pain in God's presence. Bitter tears are rooted in a sense of injustice, and are usually full of frustration. They demand an explanation. When we come into the presence of the Lord, we must be willing to let go of our sorrow. Lamentations 2:19b says, "...Pour out your heart like water before the face of the Lord. Lift your hands toward Him..." Lifting your hands is a universal sign of surrender. While you want to hold onto your right to be hurt, it will be difficult to be healed. When you surrender every ounce of pain in the presence of the Lord, He will bring lasting restoration.

Adults often tell children to dry their eyes. Crying is seen by some as soft. There is a popular myth that *real men don't cry*. This is not true. Any culture which teaches that weeping is weakness is wrong. Joseph, one of the Bible's greatest leaders, sobbed in public on several occasions. Not once did he seem ashamed or embarrassed. In fact, he cried freely and frequently - even though he was the second most powerful man in the land. It is not only Joseph who knew how to weep. We have countless biblical examples of mighty men pouring out their hearts, both in private and public. Jesus, the Lion of the tribe of Judah, wept.

SAY IT LIKE IT IS

After recovering in hospital, my American spiritual mother Cathy Lechner suddenly went downhill fast. I was about to leave home to minister at our Bible academy when her daughter Jerusha called me with the tragic news: "Mom's heart stopped beating a few minutes ago." It felt like someone had stabbed me in the chest. Nonetheless, I had to minister, so I gathered myself together, left the house, drove to our church and taught a roomful of eager students. I made my way through the time of ministry, then headed back home with a broken heart.

I have never met a more affirming human being. She was the greatest cheerleader anyone could wish to have. Not many ministers have a true mentor. I had the privilege of being coached and constantly encouraged by this unique lady. Every time I pictured her face, the pain intensified. Tears kept falling. The evening she died, my son sent me a recording of his first ever preaching. As I listened to Benj share the word of God, I felt so proud of him. All of a sudden, I cried out, "I don't want to tell You, Lord! I want to tell my mama!" (I always shared my children's milestones with Prophet Cathy because she prayed daily for them both). I fell to the floor and wept. Pain from the deep recesses of my soul streamed out as I cried before the Lord. I wept hard and loud before God. I told Him exactly what was hurting me in that moment. It was a bit brutal, but it was the truth, and it released my healing. After a while, my tears dried up and I went to bed.

The Lord can handle the truth, even if it sounds irreverent. He knows the secrets of our hearts and, as David wrote in Psalms 139:1-2 (NLT), "O Lord, you have examined my heart and know everything about me. You know when I sit down or stand up. You know my thoughts even when I'm far away." God knew David's thoughts and He knows yours and mine. God knows that I love Him with my everything, but in that moment, I did not want to share with my Heavenly Father. I wanted to talk to my spiritual mother. When I cried out that night, the words I said released a ball of pain that was bound up inside.

The following morning, I didn't hurt the way I did the day before. God had started healing me. My heart still hurt, yet not as badly as before. A week later, I was in Maryland in the US ready to run one of our Healed for Life conferences. I went for a walk early in the morning. As I worshipped, more pain surfaced so I shared my sadness with the Holy Spirit. I wept - gently this time - as I walked and talked with the Lord. This encounter was not as dramatic as the first one. However, it was just as healing. I had two other significant healing experiences in the weeks afterwards as the Lord restored me. Healing is a journey. We know when we have arrived because we don't hurt anymore. We are free.

TENDER LOVING CARE

A seriously sick patient will be treated in an intensive care unit with twenty-four-seven medical support. The Lord is watching over you, giving you the loving care that you need to bring you back to full health. Psalms 147:3 says, "He heals the brokenhearted and binds up their wounds." *Raphah*, the Hebrew for heals, is the same word that is used elsewhere in the Bible for curing physical pain. Just as the Lord wants to mend a broken arm, so He is committed to healing your broken heart. This verse goes a step further. Your Heavenly Father wants to bind up and take care of your wounds.

Let's look at the story of a Samaritan man who cared for a Jew after a brutal attack. Luke 10:30b, 33-34 reads: "A certain man went down from Jerusalem to Jericho, and fell among thieves, who stripped him of his clothing, wounded him, and departed, leaving him half dead... But a certain Samaritan, as he journeyed, came where he was. And when he saw him, he had compassion. So he went to him and bandaged his wounds, pouring on oil and wine; and he set him on his own animal, brought him to an inn, and took care of him." A man was attacked, robbed and left for dead. There is no doubt that he suffered a terrible trauma, but the tender care of the Samaritan will have restored his faith in human nature as well as his body.

This story is a picture of the way that our Heavenly Father treats us when we are in pain. Filled with compassion, He tends to the place that hurts. He gently cleanses, pouring on the ointment of His precious love, and then bandages our wounds. When your arm is broken, His power heals. When your heart is shattered, He seeks to minister to each precious piece of your heart. Psalms 34:18 (AMPC) says, "The Lord is close to those who are of a broken heart and saves such as are crushed with sorrow..." No experience is too great or too small. He is able and He is longing to make you whole again.

I SHOULD HAVE KNOWN BETTER...

As my daughter left the house, pushing her bicycle, my husband called out one last time, "Make sure you wear your helmet!" With a knowing grin, Abby replied, "Of course, Daddy!" Off she went. It was two hours later that a panicked friend of Abby's called my husband. Our daughter had been catapulted off her bicycle while heading downhill at about twenty-five miles an hour on a gravel path. By the time my husband reached the scene, the emergency services were treating Abby. Covered in blood, looking up at her father from the ambulance stretcher, my daughter managed to mumble the words, "I'm so sorry, Daddy. I wasn't wearing my helmet!"

Abby had broken her wrist and fractured her jaw in two places. Her face was torn apart by the rocks and gravel where she hit the ground. She looked like something from a horror movie. Despite the terrible pain, all that Abby could think about was that she had not worn her helmet. She was afraid that her dad would be annoyed at her for disobeying his instructions. Even though a helmet would not have helped on this occasion, she felt responsible for her injuries and expected her father to be disappointed. Of course, she could not have been more wrong. My husband was overwhelmed with compassion and did everything he could to help.

If you feel responsible for your pain, that does not mean that the Lord wants you to suffer - even for a moment. God loves you with all of His heart and wants to restore you back to health. Deuteronomy 32:10 describes the heart of God for His child: "He found him in a desert land and in the wasteland, a howling wilderness; He encircled him, He instructed him, He kept him as the apple of His eye." When you are in the wilderness - or even a self-inflicted wasteland - you are still the apple of God's eye.

THE HEART OF THE FATHER

God is not just your Lord. He is also your Heavenly Father. He loves you and wants the best for you, irrespective of the circumstances that led to your problems. You have probably heard the story that Jesus told about the prodigal son. A man had two sons and the youngest asked for his inheritance early. This was the equivalent of saying, "Dad, I wish you were dead!" Imagine the audacity it would take to ask your father to give you your inheritance while he is still alive! Well, that's what this young man did. He then blew his dad's hard-earned savings on parties and prostitutes, probably shaming the family at the same time. After the money ran out, the young man hit rock bottom and came to his senses. He decided to go home and ask to be hired as a servant in his father's house.

This young man got what he deserved, but that did not diminish his father's love. Luke 15:20 (TPT) describes what happened when he headed home: "So the young son set off for home. From a long distance away, his father saw him coming, dressed as a beggar, and great compassion swelled up in his heart for his son who was returning home. So the father raced out to meet him. He swept him up in his arms, hugged him dearly, and kissed him over and over with tender love." God will never run out of love for you. His longing is that you are restored.

At one of our events many years ago, the Lord instructed me to minister to a woman who was bound with grief and guilt after having several abortions. Following the leading of the Holy Spirit, I said something like this to her, "You and I are both grieving mothers who have lost children. The Lord wants to heal your broken heart." She broke down and sobbed, feeling permission for the first time to grieve for her lost babies. Whatever the cause, the Lord wants you to be restored.

A LIFELONG JOURNEY

Please don't assume that you are fine when you may be only *partially* healed. Jeremiah 17:9 (AMPC) says, "The heart is deceitful above all things... Who can know it [perceive, understand, be acquainted with his own heart and mind]?" Your heart will often tell you that you are okay, and that you don't need any more healing. I can't tell you how many times people have come to our events thinking that they were attending to support a friend, only to discover that they were weighed down with their own pain!

Sometimes we try to avoid the truth because it is uncomfortable. At other times, it just seems like too much work. In all honesty, pain and buried problems make life uncomfortable - not the truth. The Lord wants to bring you to a place of complete security. He wants you to enjoy enduring inner peace. This only comes as you allow God to highlight hidden hurts and reveal buried insecurities so that He can heal. He wants to take you on a journey to wholeness. He does not want you to stop until your heart is *really* restored.

Jeremiah 8:11 (NASB) says, "They heal the brokenness of the daughter of My people superficially, Saying, 'Peace, peace,' But there is no peace." Maybe a friend or family member is telling you to "Move on" and "Get over it", or perhaps you are being impatient with yourself. The Lord is not in a rush, so please take the time that you need to be fully restored. If you were encountering problems with your physical heart, I am sure that you would be diligent to get the help you needed. Although that vital organ keeps your body going, it is your inner well-being that determines what kind of life you have (see Proverbs 4:23).

Healing is a journey. In more than fifteen years of ministering to the human heart, I have never seen someone healed of every wound in one encounter. Just as we will contend with sin until we go to heaven, so you and I will have to be healed of hurts until the end of our lives. The good news is that as you get restored of the pain of the past, your life will become more enjoyable. It will become easier to be healed of day-to-day difficulties, and even of major tragedies. Before we pray, go back to your list of traumatic events at the end of section one. This is your list of difficult experiences that have affected your life. Look at your list and ask the Holy Spirit to spotlight the memories that He wants to deal with now. You can go back over your list and pray through each experience as the Spirit leads. Let's pray:

Heavenly Father,

I come before You with a wide-open heart. I recognize that You know me better than I will ever know myself. You understand everything about me. You know why I do what I do. You know my thoughts and You know what I'm going to say before I even open my mouth. You know me completely and You love me.

I ask You to shine Your light into the depths of my innermost being and reveal any hidden hurts. Bring to the surface the memories that You want to heal, Oh Lord. I surrender every corner of my heart to You and give You complete permission to do what You want to do. I ask for your help to reconnect with pain that I have pushed down. I am willing to feel so that I can be healed. Lord, I ask for your help to speak out the words that have been trapped inside.

I have been hurt, Lord. (*Now tell the Lord what you went through in as much detail as possible. He is your Wonderful Counsellor. Share what happened and also tell Him how it made you feel. Say what you have never said to anyone before.*) It was awful, Lord. I don't know why I had to suffer like that. I ask You to heal my heart, one broken piece at a time. I surrender all my sadness to You, Oh Lord. I won't turn away from my pain anymore and I won't hold onto it, either. I give You every agony, Lord.

Now I ask you to fill me afresh with Your wonderful healing presence. I receive Your anointing which soothes me deep down. I receive Your love in the depths of my heart. I receive Your enduring peace. Thank You for starting a new work in me. I ask You to continue healing me until I am made whole. I give You the praise and glory.

In Jesus' name,

Amen.

Chapter 9

FREEDOM

I became increasingly anxious when travelling on the road in America following a car crash in Atlanta. As I frequently minister in the country and am driven to different places, that was a real problem. I would find myself grabbing my seat every time the car in front braked. It reached the point where I would speak to my driver as politely as possible before we even pulled away. "It would mean so much to me if you could keep your eyes on the road. You don't need to look at me when I'm speaking. And please keep to the speed limits!"

Even when the best driver was behind the wheel, my heart would race. On one particular two-hour journey, I decided I had to conquer this fear. I turned to Scripture and a few verses jumped out at me. The Lord gave me Psalms 32:6b-7 (AMPC), which says: "... When the great waters [of trial] overflow, they shall not reach him. You are a hiding place for me; You, Lord, preserve me from trouble, You surround me with songs and shouts of deliverance. Selah [pause, and calmly think of that]!"

FIGHT FOR THE RIGHT THOUGHTS

The words of that verse started to filter through my mind, then I remembered a worship song based on the passage. I plugged headphones in my ears to block out the noise of the road, and started to sing softly in my heart. After telling the oncoming cars that they could not hurt me, I took my eyes off the traffic and gazed out of my side window at the passing scenery. I deliberately moved my attention away from the enemy's empty threats and focused on the faithfulness of my Heavenly Father. The truth that He is my protector grew inside as the enemy's lies lost their grip. This became my habit until every anxiety left. Deliberately and continuously shifting my thoughts from lies to the truth brought complete freedom.

Your thoughts are your choice. Even when your back is against a wall and it looks like there is no way out, you can decide what you allow to dominate your thoughts. Romans 12:2 (TPT) says, "Stop imitating the ideals and opinions of the culture around you, but be inwardly transformed by the Holy Spirit through a total reformation of how you think. This will empower you to discern God's will as you live a beautiful life, satisfying and perfect in his eyes." The NLT puts one phrase of Romans 12:2 like this, "Be transformed by changing the way you think." It's not easy to master your mindset, but it is essential to your well-being.

My husband and I were at a conference in central London when we received an alarming phone call about our son: "Benjy has been hit by a car. He is OK, but he is in an ambulance on his way to hospital!" The hour's drive to my six-year-old son felt like forever as I imaged how he must be feeling. He had run ahead of the babysitter and out onto the road just as a car drove around the corner. Thrown over the hood and then back down onto the ground, he was cut and bruised, but had no obvious broken bones. Doctors were assessing him for any unseen injuries. I was in a mess until I reached the hospital and saw Benjy's sweet face. I could tell he would be fine.

FIRST RESPONSE

Afterwards, I asked my husband about the incident because I noticed that he remained calm through it all. "I bound the spirit of fear immediately and then started to declare God's Word over our son," Paul explained. His first response was prayer. While I was fearing the worst, my husband was in faith and believing for the best. I was terrified. Paul was trusting. I asked the Lord to teach me how to conquer fear. Although He did not orchestrate what happened next, He used it to show me the right way to respond...

A few months later, while my son was at a party, the mother of the birthday boy called me. "Jo, I'm so sorry..." I could hear panic in Catherine's voice. "Ben has been hit by a car! I think he is OK, but I'm so sorry..." This time, I chose to be calm. I asked some key questions to establish the facts and reassured the lady that everything would be well. I did not allow my thoughts to be dominated by anxiety. I instead focused on building my faith. More often than not, fear is a waste of energy which only makes difficult situations worse. I also did what I should have done earlier and taught my son about road safety!

An important step towards freedom from fear is filtering your thoughts. When anxious ideas disturb you, don't allow them to find a home. Be conscious of what you are meditating on and be quick to catch negativity. Colossians 3:2 (MSG) says, "Don't shuffle along, eyes to the ground, absorbed with the things right in front of you. Look up, and be alert to what is going on around Christ—that's where the action is. See things from His perspective." God is bigger than the things that are bigger than you. He is your Defender. Don't allow the devil to decide what you dwell on. Instead, become deliberate about choosing your perspective. You can steer your thoughts in the right direction by refusing to dwell on anything you dread, and focus on the greatness of God. My book, My Pretend Friend, will help you to conquer your thought life.

LIAR LIAR

Faith is believing what God says, while fear is believing what the enemy says - and the devil is a liar. Speaking about satan, Jesus said in John 8:44 (NLT): "He has always hated the truth, because there is no truth in him. When he lies, it is consistent with his character; for he is a liar and the father of lies." The devil is the commander-in-chief of the domain of darkness, and fear is one of his senior servants. The threats that the enemy uses to intimidate you are not based on truth. They are a plot to cause harm.

Fear is rooted in deception. Sometimes the threats that the enemy whispers in our ears are a complete fabrication. For example, fear will make you believe that a common spider is a terrible threat. It will tell you that you can never get into a car again after that crash. It will try to convince you that the examination is too difficult. By pedaling lies like these, the devil makes you think that the challenge that you are facing is overwhelming. Fear will magnify any problem. When we separate falsehood from fear, it becomes easier to tackle and defeat.

Even when there is some factual basis for what fear says, it is still propelled by deception. For example, there is only a tiny chance that the car on the other side of the road will hit your vehicle. The call from your child's school is highly unlikely to be tragic news. You probably will succeed in that exam or business venture. AND, even if it does not work out the way you want, Jesus will never leave you nor forsake you. Fear almost always makes things worse. It hampers your ability to make good choices and gives the devil a foothold.

SILENCING SATAN

My husband's family has a history of heart disease. Paul's dad, along with several of his uncles, died of a heart attack in his early sixties. One night, my husband suffered from severe palpitations which caused his heart to beat profusely. I could feel something like a soft golf ball pounding out of the side of his ribs. Fear flooded my thoughts and drove out any faith. Jesus told a dad whose daughter was on the brink of death, "Do not be afraid, only believe." (Mark 5:36). Fear and faith are opposites, so in order to have faith, we need to drive out fear.

I realized that fear was gripping my heart. The main threat I was hearing was the suggestion that I could not survive without my husband. I stopped. I cast every anxiety on to the Lord and then I made a highly unorthodox statement: "If my husband were to die, I would get healed by my faithful God. I would help my children to be healed. I would eventually come out the other side stronger than ever." I took the lies out of the enemy's threats, confronted the devil with the truth, and fear evaporated. I then reminded myself of God's promises concerning healing. Faith arose and I prayed for my husband's health.

What has the devil been threatening *you* with? Which memories or thoughts have become objects of dread? When we are afraid of anything, from the past or in the future, we give it power in our lives. Jeremiah 42:11 says, '"Do not be afraid of the king of Babylon, of whom you are afraid; do not be afraid of him," says the LORD, "for I am with you, to save you and deliver you from his hand."' The king of Babylon was probably the most powerful man on earth at that time. Without divine intervention, he could have destroyed the Israelites. God does not want you to remain afraid of anything. In essence, that verse is saying: do not be afraid of your greatest fear!

Look at the threats that satan is waving in front of your face, grab them out of his hand and then tear them into tiny pieces. See your fears from a heavenly perspective. They are nothing before the face of the Lord. Don't be afraid of the devil's worst weapons. Even death has been defeated by the resurrection of Jesus. Paul the apostle modelled the way to overcome fear when he boldly declared, "O death, where is your victory? O death, where is your sting?" (Corinthians 15:55 NLT). If you refuse to be afraid of harm or even death (your death or the death of those you love), the devil will find it much harder to torment you.

THE LEGALIST

The devil is a liar, but he is also a legalist. He looks for legal reasons to cause further hurt. Let me explain another way that he uses fear as a weapon against you. As we expose his plots, you can arise stronger than ever. Proverbs 23:18b (KJV) says that your "... expectation shall not be cut off." This verse shows the power of expectation to bring fulfillment. The enemy knows this, so he uses fear to direct your expectations towards a negative outcome. This principle operated in Job's life. Although he was righteous man, Job never conquered intimidating thoughts. In Job 3:25, he said, "For the thing I greatly feared has come upon me, and what I dreaded has happened to me." By fearing something, we may unwittingly give the devil a legal reason to cause harm.

Fear tempts us to expect the worst, but it also tries to influence our words. Maybe you have said things like: "It's never going to happen," "I'm going to fail again," or even, "I can't take this anymore!" Proverbs 18:21 explains that, "Death and life are in the power of the tongue..." The Message translation makes this verse crystal clear: "Words kill, words give life; they're either poison or fruit—you choose." While you are filtering your thoughts, make sure you also watch your words. Jesus said that we will have what we say (see Mark 11:23b). That means that fear-filled speech has the power to cause problems. It's time to expose the liar, disarm the legalist and kick the enemy out of our lives!

THE GOOD NEWS

When Jesus went to the cross, He disarmed satan's power, and gained victory over the enemy publicly (see Colossians 2:15). He then gave you the authority that belongs to Him. You are an overcomer, but you need to take what is yours. If you were given a car which was delivered to your driveway, you would need to pick up the keys, unlock the door, and turn the ignition to drive your vehicle. Jesus has given you authority, but you need to put it into practice. God does not make you strong *for* the battle. He gives you strength *through* the battle. Using your faith to fight against fear will give you new spiritual muscles.

It's time to refuse to live in fear any longer, and instead to arise in your authority. 2 Timothy 1:7 (AMPC) says, "For God did not give us a spirit of timidity (of cowardice, of craven and cringing and fawning fear), but [He has given us a spirit] of power and of love and of calm and well-balanced mind and discipline and self-control." If we will use the power He has given us, choose love, and align our thoughts with His, we will conquer fear. You don't need to cower. You don't need to be intimidated. You don't need to listen to any more threats. This verse gives us three weapons that we can use to obliterate fear. Let's look at them, one by one.

1. YOU'VE GOT THE POWER!

Certain jobs come with a range of benefits that are part of the 'package'. For example, as well as a salary, an employee may get money for gas (if they are required to drive), a pension, and health insurance. These benefits would be detailed in the contract because they would be part of the package associated with the job. The employer would be legally bound to provide these benefits.

Power is part of the package that is given to a believer when they make Jesus Lord. When Jesus released the great commission, He told the disciples that they had authority over the enemy. You have the power! Luke 10:19 (AMPC) says, "Behold! I have given you authority and power to trample upon serpents and scorpions, and [physical and mental strength and ability] over all the power that the enemy [possesses]; and nothing shall in any way harm you."

The verse begins with the word behold, which means look or see. You need to visualize your victory. You need to allow a picture of yourself as an overcomer to grow on the inside. See yourself as fearless. The verse goes on to explain that you have total authority over all the power of the enemy. You can trample the enemy under your feet. None of his plots against you will harm you. That's the truth - not the lies that the devil pedals. See yourself as possessing the power you need to overcome every obstacle. The devil should be afraid of you, not the other way around.

2. LOVE IS THE GREATEST

My heart believed a lie for years. I shouldn't have been surprised because Jeremiah 17:9 says, "The heart is deceitful." I thought I knew myself. Unfortunately, in this area, I was wrong. For more than thirty years, I was wary of a particular lady. I would avoid seeing her or speaking to her too often. She had caused pain in the past, so I saw my avoidance strategy as a wise way of protecting myself.

During a particularly difficult season in church life, I had to fight a great deal of intimidation. It was around this time that a mutual friend was talking to this woman on the phone. To my surprise, I chipped in: "Let me say hello!" My friend passed me the phone and I enjoyed a short conversation with this lady. Later that day, I reflected on that moment and realized that I had been afraid of that woman for many years. Because I had been overcoming intimidation in other areas of my life, a previously invisible (and yet intensely uncomfortable) fear evaporated.

I began to understand a scripture that had mystified me for years: "There is no fear in love; but perfect love casts out fear, because fear involves torment. But he who fears has not been made perfect in love." (1 John 4:18). I had often wondered why the Bible said that love casts out fear when I was certain that fear could only be driven out by strong prayer in the name of Jesus! I also could not understand why being fearful could make me less loving. I was amazed at what God showed me.

Fear of being hurt usually has self-interest at the center. (Of course, there are times when fear is completely legitimate. For example, if you were being chased by an attacker, it would be appropriate to defend yourself.) However, the majority of the time, fear is self-absorbed. It makes you feel like a victim and causes you to protect yourself. It makes you afraid of the pain or problems that another person may cause. Love, in stark contrast, is otherly. When fear says, "You could hurt me," love says, "I could help you." When fear seeks to guard self, love seeks to do good for someone else. Fear is incompatible with love.

SELF AT THE CENTER

This is especially true when it comes to a fear of people's opinions. If I am intimidated by a relative or friend, I will be concerned about how they could hurt me. I might be afraid to speak up or present a differing opinion in case I am made to feel small. Fear of man is clearly self-centered, but it is also evident in other arenas. The fear I felt as a front seat passenger in America was focused on me. I was not overly concerned about my driver or the well-being of people in other vehicles. Someone who is afraid of spiders is rarely thinking about the impact that an insect might have on others. Even if you're afraid for someone you love, concern for people in the wider community is not normally at the forefront of your mind. In truth, the more we love others, the less space we will have for fear.

Let's look at 1 John 4:18a in the AMPC: "There is no fear in love [dread does not exist], but full-grown (complete, perfect) love turns fear out of doors and expels every trace of terror..." When we are filled with the love of God, fear gets driven out. When we move our thoughts from self to someone else, we will be expelling intimidation. I had not just been 'wary' of the lady that I mentioned at the start of this section. For years I had been afraid of her hurting me. When fear of that woman left, an overwhelming love for her filled my heart. I was able to minister to her and bring comfort and strength.

Love makes you victorious because love never fails (see 1 Corinthians 13:8). Next time you are afraid, draw near to God. Take your eyes off the object of your fear and shift your focus to your Heavenly Father. Rebuke the spirit of timidity, then ask the Lord to fill you with His love. It will make you a powerful force in God's kingdom. Listen to the strength in love as it is described in 1 Corinthians 13:5b,7 (AMPC) "... Love (God's love in us) does not insist on its own rights or its own way, for it is not self-seeking; it is not touchy or fretful or resentful; it takes no account of the evil done to it [it pays no attention to a suffered wrong]... Love bears up under anything and everything that comes, is ever ready to believe the best of every person, its hopes are fadeless under all circumstances, and it endures everything [without weakening]."

CLEAR YOUR HEAD

Fear clouds good judgement and overrides sensible decisions. It causes us to lose our peace and prevents rational or logical thinking. When you are free from fear, you are able to judge what is right and best. You will be able to make excellent choices and you can think clearly and logically. Let's look again at what 1 Timothy 1:7 (AMPC) says. "For God did not give us a spirit of timidity (of cowardice, of craven and cringing and fawning fear), but [He has given us a spirit] of power and of love and of calm and well-balanced mind and discipline and self-control." Jesus has paid the price for you to have a calm inner atmosphere. He was punished so that you and I could enjoy perfect peace (see Isaiah 53:5). Just as you need to rise up and take your authority, so you also need to protect your mindset.

Fear creates a frenzy, whereas we have been promised the chance to enjoy a well-balanced mind. Fear tries to force a reaction, whereas we have been given self-control and discipline. Next time fear knocks at your door and tries to influence your thinking, take charge of your thoughts and remind yourself that the Prince of Peace is the Lord of your life. Isaiah 26:3a (AMPC) says, "You will guard him and keep him in perfect and constant peace whose mind is stayed on You..." Refuse to allow fear to capture your attention anymore. Remember that you are the boss of your inner atmosphere. You choose what you allow to dominate. When you pull your thoughts back to the safety of your Heavenly Father, and remind yourself that you are a conqueror, all the agitation of anxiety will evaporate, and peace will reign again.

Although fear is your enemy, it is vital that you lower your opinion of its power. Fear wants to control you, but when you recognize that you are the boss, you will be able to put it in its rightful place. You have the tools to dismantle its grip in your life. Just like the battles we have with sin and selfishness, I think that you and I will probably have to fight fear until we graduate to glory. But that does not matter because every conquest makes us stronger. As you triumph over every type of fear and intimidation, you will also be able to lead others into their victory.

Let's pray:

Heavenly Father,

Thank You, Lord, that You have made me more than a conqueror through Christ Jesus. Please help me to become aware of any anxious or troubled thoughts so that I can be quick to drive them out. I ask You to forgive me for fearing because fear is sin. From this day forth, I refuse to accommodate fearful thinking. In the name of Jesus, I take authority once more over the spirit of fear. I take pleasure in binding and driving the spirit of fear out of my life. Go, in Jesus' mighty name!

I choose to see memories, issues, and obstacles as powerless to hurt me. (*Now look at anything that you were once intimidated by and say out loud, "I'm not scared of you anymore!"*) Thank you, Lord, that I am safe with You at my side, and I am strong because I am filled with Your Spirit. I see myself right now as a conqueror. (*Take a few minutes now to see yourself as a victor over every spiritual enemy.*)

I am so grateful that You have given me the authority and power to trample upon serpents and scorpions in the spiritual realm. Thank You that through Jesus' death on the cross, I have authority over all the power that the enemy possesses. I give You praise that nothing shall in any way harm me!

I am sorry for the times when I have been self-centered. I ask You to fill me with Your wonderful love. I take my eyes off myself and I ask You to use me to help and bless those around me. My mind is stayed on You, Oh Lord, so I thank You for giving me Your perfect peace. I declare that my heart belongs to You, Lord, and that You are my Prince of Peace forever.

I give You all the praise and glory!

In Jesus' name,

Amen.

Chapter 10

VENGEANCE

My husband Paul had a unique relationship with our first child, Naomi. Probably her favorite spot on the planet was wrapped up in his arms. It was a joy to watch them together. About four years after Naomi was suddenly taken from us, I asked Paul a bizarre question: "Do you wish that Naomi had never died?" He looked up at me, paused and then responded: "I don't know, my love." Why would I ask such an inhuman question, and why would my husband react like that? Let me explain.

After Naomi died, I felt like my heart was in a thousand pieces. I ached in places that I did not know existed. Then, as the pain weakened, I lived a kind of half-life for several months. Of course, I worked and ministered. However, when she died, something inside me died too. Naomi was our only child at the time. We had lost the sunshine of our lives as well as our role as parents. I felt as though I went from being a mummy to being a nobody. Professionals and friends alike told us that we would never get over our daughter's death. After all, she was our flesh and blood. But God had a plan...

In the weeks and months after Naomi died, the Lord did a deep work in my heart. Through a combination of supernatural encounters in the presence of the Lord *and* a deliberate decision to release pain whenever it surfaced, God restored my soul. Perhaps my most powerful healing experience was about a month after Naomi died. I was at home alone and decided it was time to tidy her toys. As I packed away her favorite playthings, pain overwhelmed me. Not knowing how to hold myself together, I cried out to God from the depths of my being: "Help!" Almost immediately, I felt a hand reach down from heaven and into my heart. My Heavenly Father pulled out my pain. Within a matter of minutes, the agony was over. I sat on my sofa exhausted and yet astonished at God's goodness.

NO MORE PAIN

Month by month, the Lord restored my heart - one piece at a time. While He was working on me, He was also healing my precious husband. By the first anniversary of Naomi's death, we were well on the way to wholeness. Within a couple of years, virtually every shred of sadness had been taken away. God does not just put a sticking plaster over brokenness. As Psalms 147:3 (AMPC) says, "He heals the brokenhearted and binds up their wounds [curing their pains and their sorrows]."

The Lord did such a complete work that eventually, neither my husband nor I even missed our precious little princess. The Hebrew word *shalom* means so much more than our English word *peace*. Shalom refers to an inner happiness and welfare, where nothing is broken or missing. When we miss someone, it is because there is still a void in our hearts. Not only is the Lord able to completely heal, He is also able to fill every empty place because He promised us perfect peace. Psalms 29:11b says, "The Lord will bless His people with peace."

Romans 8:28 (NASB) makes an extraordinary statement: "And we know that God causes all things to work together for good to those who love God, to those who are called according to His purpose." It feels acceptable to apply this verse to certain situations. For example, it is a fitting scripture to remember if you don't get into the school you wanted or if you are overlooked for a promotion. However, it seems almost grotesque to apply Romans 8:28 to trauma or tragedy. How could abuse, violence or death ever work together for good?

PAY BACK

After your heart has been healed, you will feel huge relief and you will be able to enjoy life again. However, healing and freedom are not enough! God promised that He would cause all things to work together for the good of those who love Him and are called. So how can we see good come out of tragedy? Well, there is another scripture that shows us *how* God works even terrible trauma together for good. 2 Corinthians 1:3-4 (AMPC) says, "Blessed be the God and Father of our Lord Jesus Christ... Who comforts (consoles and encourages) us in every trouble (calamity and affliction), *so that* we may also be able to comfort (console and encourage) those who are in any kind of trouble or distress, with the comfort (consolation and encouragement) with which we ourselves are comforted (consoled and encouraged) by God."

The Lord does a life-changing work in us, but it does not stop there. This verse says that after He has healed and liberated you, He will then use you to bring comfort, healing and freedom into the lives of others. Let me remind you of the question that I asked my husband: "Do you wish that Naomi hadn't died?" Our Heavenly Father healed every corner of our broken hearts, yet He did not stop there. The Lord has used us both to bring healing to countless brokenhearted people around the world. The joy of being used by God to help others made me ask that strange question, and that same joy made it hard for my husband to answer.

I like to put it this way: God turned my river of pain into a spring of healing! I cannot tell you what a privilege it is to carry an anointing that leads His precious people out of pain and into peace. If the price I had to pay was the loss of my precious child, I can honestly say that I count it as an honor. I'm certain that the devil sorely regrets the day he attacked Naomi. We will spend eternity enjoying her company. Meanwhile, down here we get to wipe the devil's nose in his failed attempts at destroying lives, marriage, and ministries. God caused Naomi's death to work together for our good, and for the good of many others.

Your Heavenly Father has a mission for your life: He wants to heal you everywhere you hurt, set you free, fill you afresh with His Spirit, and then (drum roll...) He wants to anoint you to bring restoration and liberty to others. It is a kick in the devil's teeth every time one of God's children is restored. It adds insult to satan's injury when you go a step further and become a vessel of blessing for others. Now that's what I call vengeance!

THE BOSS

Scripture makes it clear that God is the executor of vengeance. Deuteronomy 32:35 in the Message says: "I'm in charge of vengeance and payback... And the day of their doom is just around the corner, sudden and swift and sure." It is because of God's great love for you that He ensures that the devil pays for the pain that he has caused. He also promises that punishment will be swift. This is not a minor issue for the Lord. He wants you to know that the enemy will not get away with what he has done. In Isaiah 63:4a we discover how important this is to the Lord: "For the day of vengeance is in My heart..." God is committed to this.

Although vengeance belongs to the Lord, He uses us as part of His action plan. If you will make yourself available, He will recruit you as His agent. In Jeremiah 51:20, God says, "You are My battle-ax and weapons of war: for with you I will break the nation in pieces; with you I will destroy kingdoms." This Scripture reveals God as the executor of vengeance. It is also clear that He uses you and me as His instruments to hurt the enemy. There are many ways that we can become agents of vengeance. Here are a few awesome examples.

1. BLESSED IN THE MESS

Have you ever wondered why the Lord promised to give double honor to those who were once ashamed? Isaiah 61:7a says, "Instead of your shame you shall have double honor..." Again, in Isaiah

40:2, God spoke specifically about blessing those who messed up: "Speak comfort to Jerusalem, and cry out to her, that her warfare is ended, that her iniquity is pardoned; for she has received from the Lord's hand double for all her sins." Twice, God promised to give you and me a double portion of blessing after we turn away from our mistakes. I believe this is yet another example of the Lord rubbing the enemy's nose in his dirty works. The devil constantly tempts us into behavior that harms us and grieves God. However, when we return to the Lord, He lavishes us with His mercy and goodness. It blesses Him to bless us. Plus, it aggravates the enemy!

Despite being gloriously saved as a teenager, I backslid when I went away to college. I don't do anything in half measures so I fell far from the Lord and behaved in ways that must have grieved the heart of my Heavenly Father. For five years, I drank too much, smoked shady stuff, and went to all the wrong places with all the wrong people. My behavior demolished any self-esteem I once had. It left me full of shame and self-hatred.

I was strolling through a park in central London on the day that I rededicated my life to the Lord. An old church song was playing in my mind as I walked: "In my life, Lord, be glorified, be glorified..." I tutted to myself in horror, "Nothing good could ever come from my life!" But the song continued in my heart until I heard the last line: "In my life, Lord, be glorified *today*." Just enough hope was sparked on the inside of me. I said to myself, "I've got enough faith to believe that *for today*. God could somehow get some glory from me." I then turned my heart to the Lord in prayer. "If You want my life, Lord, it's all yours." That was the beginning of the rest of my life.

Several years later, after getting married and joining my husband in ministry, I preached a message in church about restoration. Two Irish ladies listened attentively as I shared how God graciously brought me back to Himself after five years of backsliding. They came to me after the service and spoke from their hearts. "We thought you were some 'goody two shoes' who had never put a foot out of line. Now that we know where you have come from, we believe that God can use us too." I was moved. I glorified God that my story had given them hope.

Since then, every time I have shared about the mayhem that was once my life, men and women have been set free from shame and condemnation. They have been encouraged to pursue their God-given destinies. My mess has become a message that has brought freedom to God's people. At the same time, it has harmed the devil's domain. The Bible shares stories about the mistakes our heroes made. We read about Abraham's lies, Moses's anger issues, King David's love for women, and Peter denying Jesus. Their falls reassure us (and every generation of Christian) that we can get back up. God's vengeance echoes through eternity.

2. TURN AROUND

I want to return to Terry's story which I shared in Chapter 6. Repeatedly raped as a teenager while he was at boarding school, buried pain in Terry's heart turned into anger. After getting married to his childhood sweetheart, Vivian, Terry took his rage out on his wife. A quiet woman with low self-esteem, Vivian endured five years of domestic violence before her husband became a Christian. Although Terry was gloriously saved, he was not yet healed. The anger still raged inside. Terry's new weapon was verbal abuse. "You're stupid," Terry would yell at Vivian. "Look at you. You're nothing!" Terry dominated his wife, and their three children were terrified of him.

When he was in his early thirties, Terry attended his first healing conference. Sitting in a small group, my husband Paul had a word of knowledge that someone was carrying the burden of painful childhood memories. For the first time in the twenty years since the assaults, Terry shared his story. He broke down and wept. That marked the start of his healing journey. On another occasion, Terry and Vivian sat with my husband and me in our home. We talked about their marriage and their past lives. Terry cried as he talked with my husband. Vivian shared her terrible pain with me.

God continued restoring Terry and Vivian over the next decade until the hidden hurts were healed. It was a great joy to see them restored. Then the celebration came when they took over the leadership of our church's marriage ministry! This once broken couple now lead a powerful ministry which brings restoration to relationships and families. Terry is head of prayer for Healed for Life and they are both leaders who are being used to bring God's healing love to the nations. Once again, the devil loses hands down!

When the devil saw a wife-beater become a marriage minister, he must have regretted the day that he tempted a man to traumatize Terry. Terry and Vivian are amongst countless living examples of 2 Corinthians 1:4 (TPT), which says, "He always comes alongside us to comfort us in every suffering so that we can come alongside those who are in any painful trial. We can bring them this same comfort that God has poured out upon us." What He did for them, He longs to do for you. As you surrender every corner of your heart to the Lord, He will do a phenomenal work in you and then He will do glorious things through you.

Listen to the turnaround in Psalms 84:5-7: "Blessed is the man whose strength is in You, whose heart is set on pilgrimage. As they pass through the Valley of Baca, they make it a spring; the rain also covers it with pools. They go from strength to strength; each one appears before God in Zion." Baca is the Hebrew for weeping, so this passage speaks of a place of pain being transformed into a spring of life. As your toughest time becomes your greatest testimony, many will be refreshed.

3. YOUR ENEMY

Our struggle is not against flesh and blood. Your enemy is never your neighbor, or the perpetrator of your trauma. Leviticus 19:18

says, "You shall not take vengeance, nor bear any grudge against the children of your people, but you shall love your neighbor as yourself: I am the Lord." In Matthew 22:37-39, Jesus taught that the entire law could be summed up in two instructions: "You shall love the Lord your God with all your heart, with all your soul, and with all your mind." This is the first and great commandment. And the second is like it: "You shall love your neighbor as yourself." It is vital that we love. That does not mean that we will trust everyone, but we must love everyone.

One of the ways that we can partner with God's vengeance plan for our lives is by loving those who caused us harm. The devil wants you to hold grudges. God wants you to let go of every ounce of anger. Jesus has a way of taking things a step further! In Matthew 5:44, He said: "But I say to you, love your enemies, bless those who curse you, do good to those who hate you, and pray for those who spitefully use you and persecute you." Did you get that? Jesus told us to love, bless, be good to, and pray for those who have caused us harm. The Greek word for love here is agape. That's the God kind of love that gives everything unconditionally, demanding nothing in return. At the very least, we can do good to those who have really hurt us by praying for God to bless them.

If you're unsure, there is a simple heart check that you can take to make certain that you have forgiven. Shut your eyes and picture the face of anyone who has hurt you. Which emotions are stirred? Do you prickle, harden, sigh - or are you able to smile inside? When you have dug out every grudge and blessed instead, your heart will be tender towards those who once caused trauma. Keep voicing your forgiveness in prayer and choosing mercy until your heart feels free. Forgiveness does not mean that you must be in close contact. It does not necessarily suggest that it is right to trust them. Yet it does allow you to love unconditionally.

4. CAUSING CONFUSION

The enemy specializes in confusion. In fact, it's one of the hallmarks of trauma. When you suffer sudden loss, horror, attack or pain, the unexpected often causes confusion. That can create chaos and bewilderment. If you have been traumatized, you can probably relate to that. Confusion is horrible, but I have some good news: you can confuse satan! During the time of King Jehoshaphat, a massive army came against the Israelites, closing in on every side. Following the leading of the Lord, Jehoshaphat sent the worship team to the front line. As they praised, God ambushed their enemies who fled in confusion! (see 2 Chronicles 20).

Psalms 149:6-9 (TPT) says, "God's high and holy praises fill their mouths, for their shouted praises are their weapons of war! These warring weapons will bring vengeance on every opposing force and every resistant power - to bind kings with chains and rulers with iron shackles. Praise-filled warriors will enforce the judgment-doom decreed against their enemies. This is the glorious honor he gives to all his godly lovers. Hallelujah! Praise the Lord!" When you praise, irrespective of your circumstances, you become a weapon of vengeance. The devil does everything he can to shut your mouth because he cannot stand the sound of praise.

For the majority of the book of Job, the devil must have thought that he had won the victory. After losing everything that mattered, Job was devastated, confused and angry. Nothing anyone said made any difference. He seemed to be inconsolable. He had lost his children in a terrible freak accident and he was very sick. Although his wife survived, she had turned on him, so I don't think his marriage was a safe place. Everything that could possibly go wrong for Job had gone wrong. Despite his desperate circumstances, things started to turn around when Job gave glory to God. He didn't praise the Lord for the state of his life. He glorified God for His magnificence and excellence.

Job praised before he saw any change. He praised God because God deserves to be praised, and praise paved the way for his breakthrough. We don't always get to choose the outcome of the circumstances of our lives. We can choose to praise anyway. We prove our love by the way we behave in the worst circumstances. Praise is an acknowledgement that God is great, irrespective of the details of our lives. We don't need to search for reasons to worship. We can give Him glory just because He is the Lord of all.

DO PERPETRATORS PAY?

Our God is rich in mercy, but He reigns with justice. Deuteronomy 32:4 (NLT) says, "He is the Rock; his deeds are perfect. Everything he does is just and fair. He is a faithful God who does no wrong; how just and upright he is!" Everything your Heavenly Father does is just and fair. We will all face two judgements. The first will open the doors of heaven for followers of Jesus. The second judgement will be in heaven. That is when every believer will give an account for their words and deeds (see Matthew 12:36). Everyone will stand before God and give an account. However, it is not worth worrying about how someone else will be judged. It is probably more useful to focus on fulfilling your own purpose.

As well as judgement, we all operate within the laws of sowing and reaping. Galatians 6:7 (AMPC) unpacks the principle: "Do not be deceived and deluded and misled; God will not allow Himself to be sneered at (scorned, disdained, or mocked by mere pretensions or professions, or by His precepts being set aside.) [He inevitably deludes himself who attempts to delude God.] For whatever a man sows, that and that only is what he will reap." You don't need to be concerned that people who have done wrong will escape. We all reap what we sow. That's a very good reason why you should pray for those who have hurt you. They probably need your merciful petitions.

God loves every single one of us. After all, He is Creator of all. When I'm upset with someone, I remind myself that he or she is also God's child. We need to be careful how we treat His creatures! Having said that, Romans 12:19 (NLT) is clear, "Dear friends, never take revenge. Leave that to the righteous anger of God. For the Scriptures say, 'I will take revenge; I will pay them back,' says the Lord." I encourage you to take your eyes off flesh and blood, and instead determine that the devil will pay for all the pain that you have suffered.

A HEAVENLY PERSPECTIVE

In the West, it is easy to become self-absorbed. Everything around us exists to make our lives more comfortable and convenient. When we suffer, we often have a sense of injustice. In contrast, our ancestors lived with hardship and disappointment, and yet pressed on anyway. Our attitude can hold us back. If we will lift up our eyes and see a bigger picture, it will not only help us to overcome the injustice of trauma. It will pave the way for us to participate in God's vengeance plan. I encourage you to ask the Lord to use you to avenge the enemy for every agony you have suffered.

In Numbers 31:2, God instructed Moses to pay back the enemy for hurting His people: "Take vengeance on the Midianites for the children of Israel." The Lord took it personally when the devil attacked His people. In the same way, He wants the enemy to regret the day he hurt you. God can make you a thorn in the devil's side if you will ask the Lord to use your life to help others who have suffered. When you become a source of hope to the hopeless or a promise of healing to the broken, you will start to see God's vengeance plan unfold.

A couple of years after Naomi died, I met a woman who lost her six-year-old son. After our time together, she said to me, "I now have hope for the future. I now know that my heart can be made whole." I wept with joy as I made my way home. That was the first time that my story of loss and restoration helped someone who had travelled a similar journey. I was deeply moved to see hope grow in this lady's heart. You can know that same joy as God uses you.

Psalms 58:10 says, "The righteous shall rejoice when he sees the vengeance; he shall wash his feet in the blood of the wicked." We know our struggle is not against flesh and blood, but against our invisible enemy who is responsible for every calamity. The blood that we wash our feet in is therefore metaphorical. However, I promise you, it feels good to make the devil pay. I love to see souls saved, bodies healed, and faith grow. But I cannot begin to describe the joy I feel when a broken heart is healed! The enemy's plan for my demise was to ruin my life through rejection and tragedy. He failed! The Lord now uses my life to carry out His vengeance plan.

TRUE ABUNDANCE

The devil's mandate is to hurt Christians and to prevent them from fulfilling their purpose. That is what he wants to accomplish in your life. John 10:10 (AMPC) says, "The thief comes only in order to steal and kill and destroy. I came that they may have and enjoy life, and have it in abundance (to the full, till it overflows)." The devil may have hurt you in terrible ways. However, he does not have the power to stop you becoming a force for good in God's kingdom. As you arise and make yourself available to the Lord, you will be able to do great damage to the devil's domain. Jesus came to give you an abundant life, full of joy and fulfillment. Seeing the traumas of your life turned around for good is one sure way to experience that life of abundance that Jesus promised.

The devil tries to taunt you, yet you have the opportunity to make him squirm instead. Micah 7:8 says, "Do not rejoice over me, my enemy; when I fall, I will arise; when I sit in darkness, the Lord will be a light to me." It does not matter how many times you fall flat on your face, because you have the power to arise again. There is no mess, no mistake, no tragedy, no trauma that God cannot turn around for good. When you won't allow the devil to keep you down, you become unstoppable. When you surrender your heart, every source of sadness and sense of injustice, God will use you in the most remarkable way. There is something so sweet about becoming part of God's vengeance plan. You can partner with the Holy Spirit to make sure that the pain of your past comes back to haunt satan, again and again. Let's pray:

Heavenly Father,

I am so grateful to You for healing hidden hurts in my heart and for bringing me into freedom. I will stay on my journey until You lead me to wholeness. I am very grateful for You faithfulness, but Lord, I want more! Today, I ask that You will use my life and my story as part of your vengeance plan. Lord, I ask that You would use me to hurt the devil.

I surrender every ounce of sadness in my heart. I will not hold back. I ask You to continue healing me anywhere I hurt. I let go of all my pain and I ask You, the Father of all comfort, to use me to carry comfort to anyone who is hurting. Take my trauma, take my story, and use me to bring relief to others when they are in need. Make me a vessel of Your love, Your healing, Your kindness.

I surrender every mistake I have ever made and every mess in my life. I ask You to turn my life around and use my story as an encouragement to those who are weighed down with shame or condemnation. No longer will I hide my shortcomings. Instead, I give You permission to use my slips to help others get back up.

Help me, Lord, to forgive those who have hurt me. I am not their judge. You alone, O Lord, are judge. I choose to let go of every sense of injustice and every wrong. I lay it all down in Your presence. I choose mercy! Lord, I want to go a step further to make satan pay. I therefore ask You to fill me with Your unconditional love for those who made my life difficult. Help me to see them the way You do and to love them from my heart because they are Your creation.

From this day forth, I will treat my heart like the treasure that it is. I will remember that my life and all my relationships are affected by the condition of my soul.

I will praise You because You are God, because You are awesome, because You are the Lord of all. I give You glory because You deserve all glory and honor and praise! I take my eyes off my little life and I ask that You give me a heavenly perspective from this day forth.

I declare that the devil will regret the day that he hurt me because my life will bring healing and freedom to others. My story will give glory to You, Oh Lord!

In Jesus' name, I pray,

Amen.

WHAT NEXT?

Your heart is probably your most valuable, and yet your most vulnerable, asset. This book is just part of your journey to wholeness and freedom. As you finish this book, make the decision to continue to prioritize your inner wellbeing. Visit our website JoNaughton.com to find out about our range of resources to help you to wholeness. We have a mentoring network, online courses and a range of print, digital, and audio books. We run half day, full day and two-day events all designed to help you on your journey. Above all, look after your heart every day of your life for it determines the course of your life.

"I am convinced and sure of this very thing, that He Who began a good work in you will continue until the day of Jesus Christ (right up to the time of His return), developing [that good work] and perfecting and binging it to full completion in you." (Philippians 1:6 AMP)

Let that word sink deep into you. God is preparing you for your destiny. He has already started the job and He will be faithful to finish it.

AN INVITATION

If you would like to ask Jesus to become the Lord of your life, I would be honored to lead you in a simple prayer. The Bible says that God loves you and that Jesus wants to draw close to you: "Behold I stand at the door and knock. If anyone hears My voice and opens the door, I will come in." (Revelation 3:20). If you would like to know Jesus as your Friend, your Savior and your Lord, the first step is to ask. Pray this prayer:

Dear Lord,

I know that You love me and have a wonderful plan for my life. I ask You to come into my heart today and be my Savior and Lord. Forgive me for all my sins, I pray. Thank You that because You died on the cross for me, I am forgiven of every wrong I have ever committed when I repent. I give my life to You entirely and ask You to lead me in Your ways from now on.

In Jesus' name,

Amen.

If you have prayed this prayer for the first time, it will be important to tell a Christian friend what you prayed and to find a good church. Just as a newborn baby needs nourishment and care, so you (and all Christians) need the support of other believers as you start your new life as a follower of Jesus Christ.

You can watch free Bible messages that will help to build your faith by subscribing to my YouTube channel and to Harvest Church London's YouTube channel. You can follow me on Instagram (@naughtonjo), go on Facebook and like my public page (Jo Naughton), and follow me on Twitter (@naughtonjo). God bless you!

ABOUT THE AUTHOR

Jo Naughton is the founder of Whole Heart Ministries which is dedicated to helping people be free to fulfill their God-given purpose. Together with her husband Paul, Jo pastors Harvest Church in London, England. A public relations executive turned pastor, Jo's previous career included working for Prince Charles as an executive VP of his largest charity. After reaching the pinnacle of the public relations world, Jo felt the call of God to full-time ministry. She is a regular guest on TV and radio shows in the US and UK.

An international speaker and author, Jo ministers with a heart-piercing anointing, sharing with great personal honesty in conferences and at churches around the world. Her passion is to see people set free from all inner hindrances so that they can fulfill their God-given destiny. Countless people have testified to having received powerful and life-changing healing through her ministry. Jo and Paul have two wonderful children, Ben and Abby.

You can connect with Jo via:

JoNaughton.com

Instagram (@naughtonjo)

YouTube (Jo Naughton)

Facebook (public page - Jo Naughton)

Twitter (@naughtonjo)

For more information about Harvest Church London, visit harvestchurch.org.uk

ALSO BY THE AUTHOR:

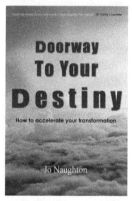

All Jo Naughton's books are available at: JoNaughton.com

CPSIA information can be obtained
at www.ICGtesting.com
Printed in the USA
LVHW070416160623
749660LV00005B/272